for
Materials
with
8-9
year olds

William Hartley

Published by Scholastic Ltd,
Villiers House,
Clarendon Avenue,
Leamington Spa,
Warwickshire CV32 5PR
Visit our website at www.scholastic.co.uk

Printed by Alden Group Ltd, Oxford

© 2002 Scholastic Ltd
Text © 2002 William Hartley

1234567890 2345678901

AUTHOR
William Hartley

LITERACY CONSULTANT
Gill Matthews

EDITOR
Joel Lane

ASSISTANT EDITOR
David Sandford

SERIES DESIGNER
Rachael Hammond

DESIGNER
Paul Roberts

COVER PHOTOGRAPH
© Stockbyte

ILLUSTRATIONS
Kirsty Wilson

British Library Cataloguing-in-Publication Data
A catalogue record for this book is available from the British Library.

ISBN 0-439-01880-3

Designed using Adobe Pagemaker

The right of William Hartley to be identified as the Author of this work has been asserted by him in accordance with the Copyright, Designs and Patents Act 1988.

All rights reserved. This book is sold subject to the condition that it shall not, by way of trade or otherwise, be lent, hired out or otherwise circulated without the publisher's prior consent in any form of binding or cover other than that in which it is published and without a similar condition, including this condition, being imposed upon the subsequent purchaser.

No part of this publication may be reproduced, stored in a retrieval system, or transmitted, in any form or by any means, electronic, mechanical, photocopying, recording or otherwise, without the prior permission of the publisher. This book remains copyright, although permission is granted to copy those pages indicated as photocopiable for classroom distribution and use only in the school which has purchased the book, or by the teacher who has purchased this book and in accordance with the CLA licensing agreement. Photocopying permission is given for purchasers only and not for borrowers of books from any lending service.

CONTENTS

5 Introduction
6 Word list

7 Comparing things ...... (recount)

8 Comparing things questions...... (higher level)
9 Comparing things questions...... (lower level)
10 What's it made of? ...... (survey)
11 Properties crossword...... (word building)
12 True or false?...... (sorting statements)
13 Guess what?...... (matching materials to descriptions)
14 What's it like?...... (matching materials to properties)

15 Materials are useful ...... (argument)

16 Materials are useful questions...... (higher level)
17 Materials are useful questions...... (lower level)
18 Sort out...... (chart filling)
19 What's it made of? ...... (matching words to pictures)
20 Materials crossword...... (crossword)
21 Match it...... (matching materials to descriptions)
22 What else would do? ...... (labelling)

23 Keeping warm ...... (report)

24 Keeping warm questions...... (higher level)
25 Keeping warm questions...... (lower level)
26 How hot is it? ...... (reading thermometer scales)
27 Reading results...... (graph analysis)
28 Looking for differences...... (explaining results)
29 Finding differences...... (investigation)
30 Report sheet...... (reporting on an investigation)

31 Materials and electricity ...... (instructions)

32 Materials and electricity questions...... (higher level)
33 Materials and electricity questions...... (lower level)
34 Cut and place...... (practical sorting)
35 Cut and paste chart...... (practical sorting)
36 Electrical facts...... (cloze passage and sorting)

37 Magnetic materials ...... (report)

38 Magnetic materials questions...... (higher level)
39 Magnetic materials questions...... (lower level)
40 Magnetic snap 1...... (card game)
41 Magnetic snap 2...... (card game)
42 Is it attracted?...... (investigation)

43 Rocks and soils ...... (information)

44 Rocks and soils questions...... (higher level)
45 Rocks and soils questions...... (lower level)
46 Looking at rocks...... (investigation)
47 Hidden rocks...... (vocabulary activity)
48 Facts about soil...... (matching sentence beginnings to endings)
49 What is soil made of?...... (deduction and explanation)
50 Down to Earth clues!...... (vocabulary game)

51 Types of change ...... (explanation)

52 Types of change questions...... (higher level)
53 Types of change questions...... (lower level)
54 What will happen?...... (reasoning, investigation)
55 Changes...... (assorted activities)
56 Changing shape...... (writing crossword clues)

CONTENTS

57 Heating and cooling ...... *(explanation)*
58 Heating and cooling questions...... *(higher level)*
59 Heating and cooling questions...... *(lower level)*
60 What will happen if...?...... *(filling in a table)*
61 Expansion and contraction...... *(cloze sentences)*
62 Temperature squares...... *(word building)*

63 Soluble or insoluble? ...... *(recount)*
64 Soluble or insoluble questions...... *(higher level)*
65 Soluble or insoluble questions...... *(lower level)*
66 Missing words...... *(cloze text)*
67 Definitions...... *(dictionary work)*
68 Dissolving times...... *(investigation)*

69 Separating mixtures ...... *(instructions)*
70 Separating mixtures questions...... *(higher level)*
71 Separating mixtures questions...... *(lower level)*
72 Sorting solids by size...... *(assorted activities)*
73 Filtering...... *(assorted activities)*
74 Separating questions...... *(knowledge-based activities)*

75 Test it ...... *(recount)*
76 Test it questions...... *(higher level)*
77 Test it questions...... *(lower level)*
78 Soaking it up...... *(investigation)*
79 Testing tights...... *(analysing data)*
80 A material test...... *(grouping materials)*

81 Water and the water cycle ...... *(explanation)*
82 Water and the water cycle questions...... *(higher level)*
83 Water and the water cycle questions...... *(lower level)*
84 The water cycle...... *(labelling)*
85 Evaporating and condensing...... *(vocabulary activity)*
86 Dirty water 1...... *(matching pictures to captions)*
87 Dirty water 2...... *(descriptive writing)*
88 Save it...... *(making an information poster)*

89 Solids and liquids ...... *(report)*
90 Solids and liquids questions...... *(higher level)*
91 Solids and liquids questions...... *(lower level)*
92 Solids and liquids pictures...... *(practical sorting)*
93 Solids and liquids chart...... *(practical sorting)*
94 Solids and liquids round-the-class game...... *(linking questions to answers)*
95 What are solids, liquids and gases?...... *(identifying correct answers)*
96 Uses of solids, liquids and gases...... *(matching materials to uses)*

INTRODUCTION

Children often struggle to remember science words. Sometimes the words seem strange, or have other meanings in everyday life. Think about these science words: *material, property, hard*. If you ask a child what these words mean, you are likely to get responses such as: 'My coat is made of material'; 'My things are my property'; 'These sums are too hard for me'. But when children go into science lessons, we sometimes assume that they already understand a 'material' to be any substance, a 'property' to be how a material behaves, and 'hard' to be a property of some materials.

Scientific language

This series aims to give children practice in using science words, both through science activities and in 'real life' contexts, so that they become familiar with the meanings of these words. Use of correct scientific vocabulary is essential for high attainment in national assessment tests. The QCA *Scheme of Work for Science* for Key Stages 1 and 2 in England suggests examples of vocabulary for each of its units; although these books are not divided into exactly the same topics, the QCA vocabulary and its progressive introduction are used as the basis for the word selection here.

The science covered is divided into units based on topics from the national curricula for England, Wales, Scotland and Northern Ireland. In this book, the science is drawn from the 'Materials and their properties' statements for ages 8–9 relating to grouping materials and changing materials. The series of boxed letters at the bottom of each page shows in which curriculum documents the focus of each activity occurs. If all the boxes are shaded like this, E NI W S (as for example on page 13), this indicates that the activity focuses on a topic from the National Curricula for England, Northern Ireland, Wales and the Scottish Guidelines.

Science and literacy

The National Literacy Strategy for England suggests teaching objectives and gives examples of the types of activities that children should encounter during each year of primary school. This book uses many of these techniques for developing children's understanding and use of scientific language. The activities here are mainly intended for use in science time, as they have been written with science learning objectives in mind. However, some of the activities could be used in literacy time. Science texts have already been published for use in literacy time, but many of them use science content appropriate for older children. During literacy time you need to be focusing on language skills, not teaching new science. It is with this in mind that these sheets, drawing from age-appropriate science work, have been produced. It is also suggested that these sheets are used in literacy time only after the science content has been introduced in science time.

The series focuses mainly on paper-based activities to develop scientific language, but it is hoped that teachers might also use some of the ideas in planning practical science activities.

About this book

Each unit in this book begins with a non-fiction text that introduces some key scientific vocabulary. The key words are highlighted by bold type. The texts cover a range of non-fiction genres. Following this text are two comprehension activities that help children to identify and understand the key words. They are pitched at two levels:

 for older or more able children

 for younger or less able children.

Although the comprehension activities are designed to be used mainly during science time, you may wish to use the texts as examples of non-fiction texts in literacy time. The comprehension pages contain two or three types of question (a change of icon indicates a change in the type of question):

 The answer can be found in the text.

 Children will need to think about the answer. These questions usually elicit science understanding beyond what the text provides.

 An activity aimed at developing the children's broader skills. These are optional extension activities for individual or group work, with teacher support if necessary.

Following the comprehension pages in each unit are activities aimed at developing children's understanding and use of the key vocabulary and additional science vocabulary. Strategies used include: making and completing diagrams, charts and tables: word building: description; matching pictures and writing; labelling; sequencing; analysing graphs and tables; matching sentence starters to endings; identifying true and false statements; word grids and wordsearches; crosswords; matching words and meanings; making connections; picture interpretation; vocabulary games and quizzes; and some easily set up practical activities.

WORD LIST

absorbent	electrical	limestone	see-through
air	insulator	liquid	separate
air spaces	electricity	magnet	shampoo
air temperature	evaporate	magnetic	shape
aluminium	expand	magnetised	shelter
appearance	experiment	magnetism	sieve
attracted	explained	manufactured	slate
bar magnet	fall	marble	sleet
bend	feather	material	snow
boiling point	filter paper	measure	soak
boulder	flexible	melt	soaked
brick	flow	melting	soil
burning	force	mixture	solid
chart	fossil	natural	soluble
change	freeze	natural gas	steel
cloud	freezing	naturally	stick to
coal	freezing point	non-magnetic	stone
compare	funnel	odour	table
concrete	fur	particle	temperature
condense	glass	pebble	texture
contract	granite	plastic	thermal
cooking oil	grit	poured	insulator
cool	hail	process	thermometer
cooled	hair	properties	transparent
cotton	heat	rain	volume
crust	heated	record	warm
degrees Celsius	humus	rice	warmth
dissolve	ice	rise	water
droplet	insoluble	rock	water cycle
dropper	instrument	rubber	water vapour
edible	insulating	salt	wood
electrical	properties	sand	wooden
conductor	iron	scale	wool

Comparing things

This morning, our class found out about the **properties** of six different **materials**. It was part of a science topic we are doing to help us understand why some materials are better than others for certain jobs.

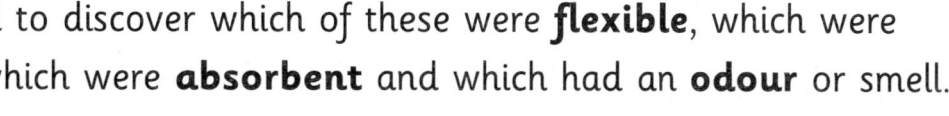

The materials we tested today were glass, rubber, clear plastic film, cork, Plasticine and sponge. We had to discover which of these were **flexible**, which were **transparent**, which were **absorbent** and which had an **odour** or smell.

First we held each material in turn in both hands and tried to **bend** it. The rubber, clear plastic, cork, Plasticine and sponge would all bend quite easily. These materials were **flexible**.

Then we tried to **see through** each material. We could see through the glass and the clear plastic. These materials were **transparent**.

We put five droplets of water from a **dropper** onto the surface of each material. The droplets **soaked** into the cork and the sponge. These materials were **absorbent**.

Finally, we smelt each material to find out whether it had an **odour**. The rubber and the Plasticine had a strong odour. The other materials did not.

When we had finished carrying out our tests, we wrote our results in a **table**.

Comparing things

1. Name the **materials** that the children tested. _____
   _____

2. Complete this sentence with a list.
   The materials were tested to discover which of them were:

   • _____   • _____

   • _____   • _____

3. Describe how the children found out whether a material was **flexible**.
   _____
   _____

4. Which materials were smelly? _____

5. Write the names of the materials that were **opaque**.
   _____

6. Which material tested was **rigid**? _____

7. Fill in this table to show what the children discovered.
   One column has been done for you.

flexible	transparent	absorbent	smelly
		cork sponge	

On another piece of paper, write down the meanings of these words:

   flexible   transparent   rigid   absorbent   odour

Check your meanings by looking in a dictionary.

Comparing things

1. Name three of the **materials** the children tested.

   _____   _____   _____

2. Cross out the *incorrect* words in this sentence.
The materials were being tested to see whether they were **strong / flexible / transparent / tough / smooth / absorbent / hard / smelly**.

3. Which **property** of each material did the children test first?

   _____

4. Write the names of the two **transparent** materials.

   _____   _____

5. Which materials had a **smell**?

   _____

6. Find out the names of two other **absorbent** materials that are not mentioned in the text. Write them here.

   _____   _____

7. All the materials had one **property** in common. Write it here.

   ƒ_____

8. Tick the word that might describe clear plastic.

   ☐ table   ☐ properties   ☐ smell   ☐ transparent
   ☐ soaked   ☐ dropper   ☐ odour   ☐ materials

On another sheet of paper, write down the meanings of these words:

   flexible   transparent   absorbent   odour

Check your meanings by looking in a dictionary.

What's it made of?

Survey your school to find out what materials the different parts of the building are made of. Fill in this **chart**. One example has been done for you.

Building feature	Made from	Why it was made from that material							
window	glass	Glass is rigid, smooth, transparent and waterproof, and it lasts a long time.							

Properties crossword

All these words describe materials.
Write them on the crossword in their correct places.

smell	liquid	flexible	dull	stretchy
runny	elastic	absorbent	tough	solid
texture	opaque	jagged	brittle	hard

True or false?

In each pair of sentences, only one sentence is true. Underline this sentence, then rewrite the false sentence on another sheet of paper to make it true.

The way a material looks is called its **appearance**.
Solids are **sloppy**, but most liquids are **firm**.

A **stiff** material will bend or change its shape easily.
Sand and gravel will **sink** when put in a bowl of water.

A **smooth** surface is bumpy and uneven.
Wood and cork will **float** near the surface of water.

Similar materials are very much alike.
When something is **squashed** it always stays the same shape.

Solid materials **flow** quite easily.
When melted, ice turns into a **fluid**.

Different materials can sometimes be used to make **similar** objects.
A **natural** material is one that has been made by humans.

Waterproof materials do not let water pass through them.
Materials that are **weak** do not break easily.

An object that is **soft** is firm and stiff.
A **manufactured** material is one that has been made by humans.

Guess what?

Match each description with the most suitable **material**. Choose the material from the word list and write its name in the answer box next to its description.

Be careful! Read all the descriptions before you start writing. Use a dictionary and other reference books to help you.

1.	brittle, hard, transparent	1.	
2.	soft, stretchy, natural fibres	2.	
3.	liquid, colourless, tasteless	3.	
4.	edible, granular, dissolves in water	4.	
5.	hard, rough, building material	5.	
6.	liquid, smooth, lubricant	6.	
7.	tough, strong, manufactured fibres	7.	
8.	runny, sticky, produced by bees	8.	
9.	strong, hard, goes rusty	9.	
10.	yellowish, edible, greasy	10.	
11.	waterproof, smooth, made into candles	11.	
12.	tough, elastic, made into balloons	12.	
13.	liquid, white, cows produce it	13.	
14.	metal, will not go rusty	14.	
15.	black, absorbent, used for drawing	15.	
16.	flat, flexible, often white	16.	

rubber   milk   rock   honey   paper   glass
oil   aluminium   wax   wool   butter
iron   water   nylon   charcoal   sugar

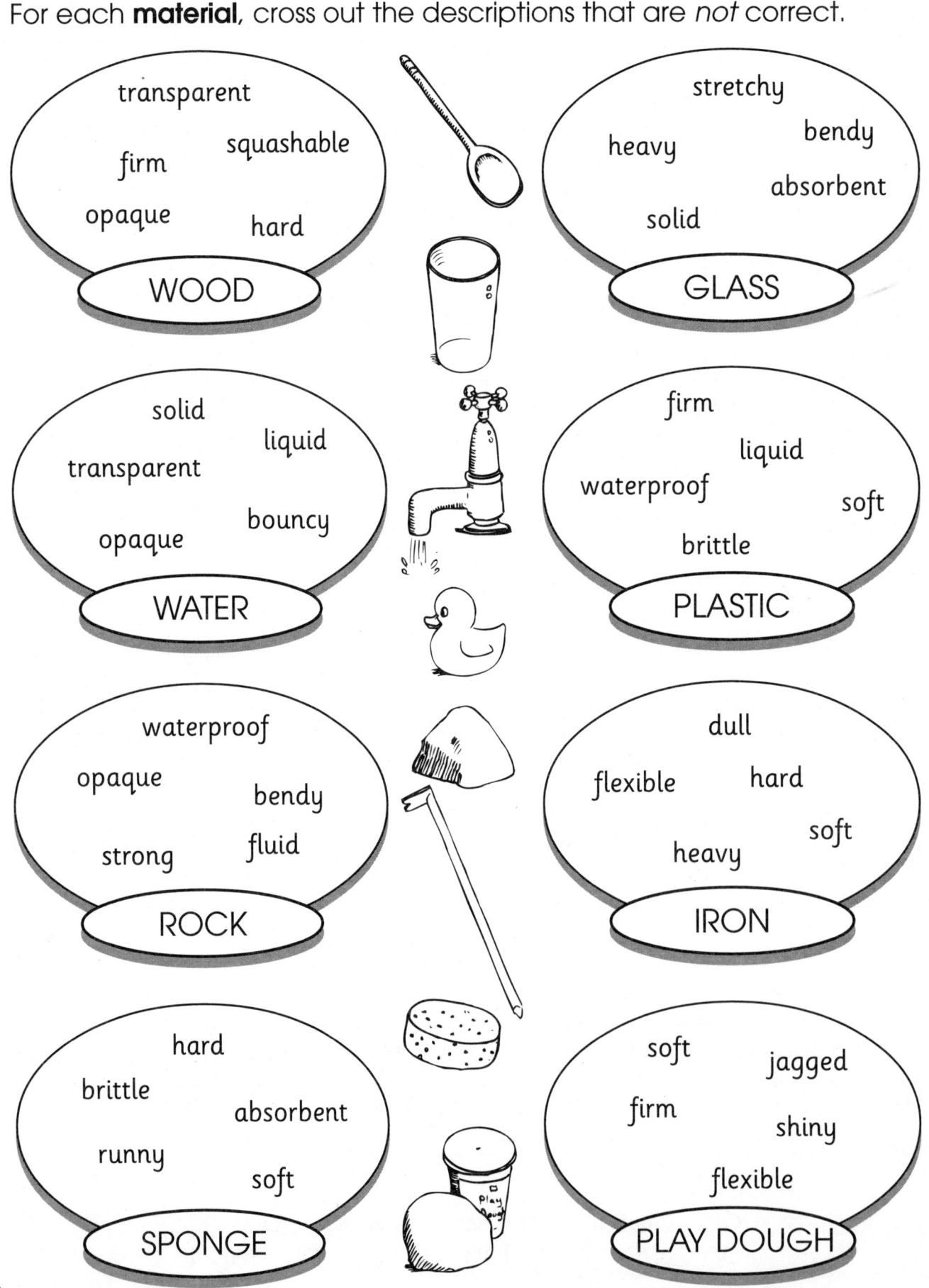

Materials are useful

To stay alive, humans have to use many different **materials**. Some of these materials occur **naturally**, but others have to be **manufactured**.

Some materials provide us with food. These are called **edible** materials. Edible materials, such as bread, meat, potatoes and pasta, usually come from plants and animals.

There are other materials that are not edible. Some of these can be used to supply **warmth** and **shelter**. For example, **coal** and **natural gas** provide the energy we need for cooking food and supplying heat to homes, schools and places of work.

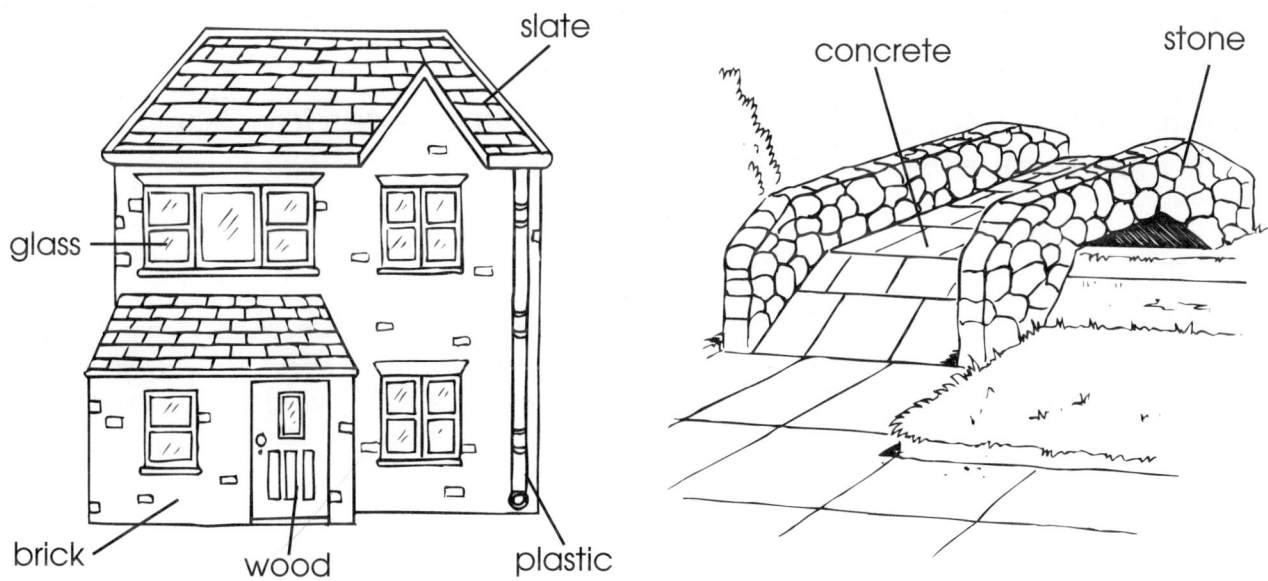

Stone, **brick**, **slate** and **concrete** are materials used for building houses, factories, bridges and tunnels. **Glass**, **wood** and **plastic** are other important materials used in all kinds of building work.

Look around your classroom. How many different kinds of materials are there? They are all useful to us.

Photocopiable

Materials are useful

1. Answer each question with a complete sentence.

   • What are the two main types of material?

   _____

   • What are the materials called that provide us with food?

   _____

   • Name one way in which **coal** and **natural gas** are useful to us.

   _____

2. Name four things that **stone**, **brick**, **slate** and **concrete** can be used to build.

   _____

3. Tick the materials that might also be useful in building work.

   glass ☐   humus ☐   plastic ☐   wood ☐   peat ☐

4. Write the names of three materials you ate yesterday that are not mentioned in the text.

   _____   _____

5. Shade the names of **manufactured** materials in this list.

   | glass | stone | brick | slate | concrete | wood | plastic |

6. Name two things in your classroom that are made out of **plastic**. Next to each name, write a different material it could have been made from.

7. Ring the materials that are mixed together to make **concrete**.

   plaster   sand   flax   soil   gravel   cement

What do you think is the most useful material in the world? On another sheet of paper, write its name and why you have chosen it. Do not choose a kind of food.

Materials are useful

1. Fill in the missing words in these sentences.

   • Some materials occur _____.

   • Some materials have to be _____.

   • _____ materials provide us with food.

2. Ring the **edible** materials in this list.

   potato   wool   bread   pasta   rubber   meat

3. Which materials provide the energy we need for cooking food and heating our homes? _____

4. Write the names of four important building materials.
   _____

5. Draw three **edible** materials you ate yesterday that are not mentioned in the text. Write their names underneath.

6. **Glass** is a **manufactured** material. Write the names of two other manufactured materials.
   _____
   _____

7. Complete this sentence:
   Some bottles are made of **plastic** because _____
   _____

Discuss with a friend what you think is the most useful material in the world. Write down five of its uses. Do not choose a kind of food.

Photocopiable

Sort out

Some of the things we use are made from **natural** materials. Others are made from materials that have to be **manufactured**.

Look at these pictures of different objects. Under each picture is the name of the material from which it is made. Copy each name into the correct box below.

natural			
	glass	cork	paper
	nylon	fibre glass	cardboard
	charcoal	wool	wood
clay	cotton	marble	manufactured
plastic	iron	polythene	
card	granite	leather	

SCHOLASTIC DEVELOPING SCIENCE LANGUAGE for Materials with 8–9 year olds

What's it made of?

Some **materials** are better than others for the jobs they do.

1. Label this picture of a car, using the words **metal**, **glass**, **plastic** and **fabric**.
On another sheet of paper, write why each material is used where it is in the car. Use the words **strong**, **transparent**, **flexible** and **soft**.

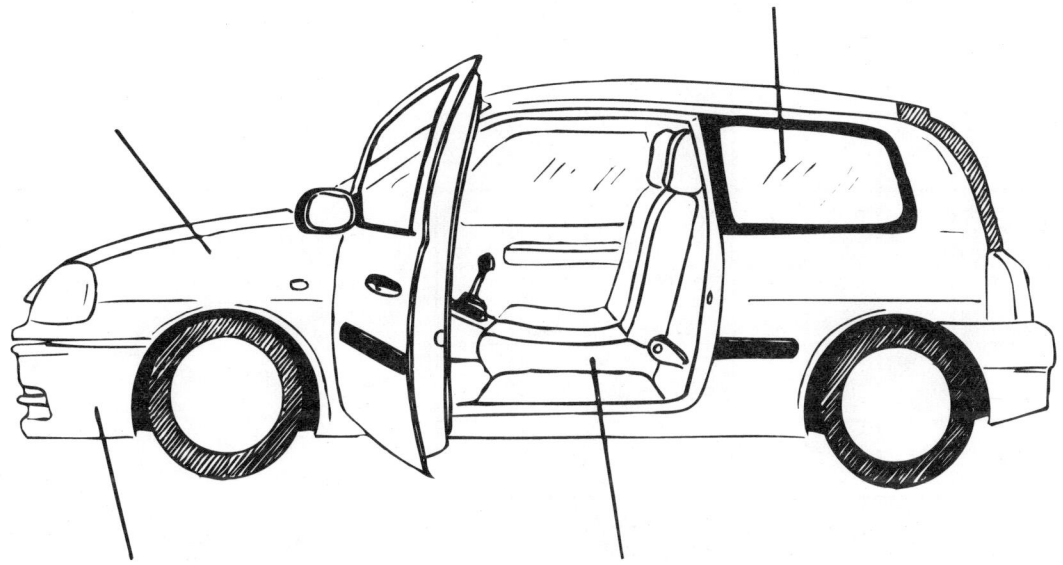

Sometimes things are made from a **mixture** of materials.

2. Draw a line from each item to the pair of materials it is most likely to be made from.

plastic and metal	book	graphite and wood
	light switch	
	pencil	
rubber and leather	shoe	paper and glue

3. Write the title **Fantastic Plastic** at the top of a large sheet of paper. Draw and name the things in your classroom that you would have to do without if plastic had not been invented.

Materials crossword

All of the answers in this crossword are the names of **materials**. The words across have been written for you.

The words down the crossword still have some letters missing. Use the 'Down' clues to help you complete these words.

```
1S A 2N D S T 3O N E
4L  I Q U I 5D
         6I R O N
                    7
      8
9C H A R C O A L
         10L E A D
                11B O N E
```

Down

1. A type of material that does not flow.
2. A mixture of flour and water used for making bread.
3. A tough and strong manufactured fibre.
5. A very hard, brilliant and valuable kind of stone.
7. A hard rock from which statues are often made.
8. Frozen raindrops.
9. The light, tough bark of a kind of oak tree.

On another sheet of paper, write a set of clues for the words across the crossword. Make your clues accurate but quite short, like the ones above. Use a dictionary to help you.

Match it

Draw a line to join each **material** to the set of **properties** that describe it.

- burns easily
- goes soggy when wet
- used to make boxes

- tough and flexible
- made from a natural source
- used to make shoes, handbags and gloves

- a metal
- light in weight
- sometimes used for drinks cans

- a natural material
- often cut into planks
- used to make sheds, doors and furniture

- moves by flowing
- smooth and slippery
- used as a fuel

aluminium
oil
sugar
leather
wood
salt
glass
wool
brick
cardboard

- smooth and transparent
- made from sand
- used to make windows

- obtained from a plant
- bad for your teeth
- used as a sweetener

- a rough texture
- baked clay
- used for building houses

- found in sea water
- you can tell it by its taste
- can be used on your dinner!

- soft, stretchy fibres
- grown by an animal
- used to make warm clothes

Photocopiable

What else would do?

Look at the picture below. From the list of words, choose the best **material** for each part of the house. Write it in the first box of each pair.

| glass | brick | concrete | plastic | wood | slate |

glass	Perspex

For each material you have named, think of a **different** material that could be used instead. Write the name of that material in the second box. Do not choose any materials that have already been used.

An object is not always made from the **same** material. Write the names of two different materials that each object could be made from.

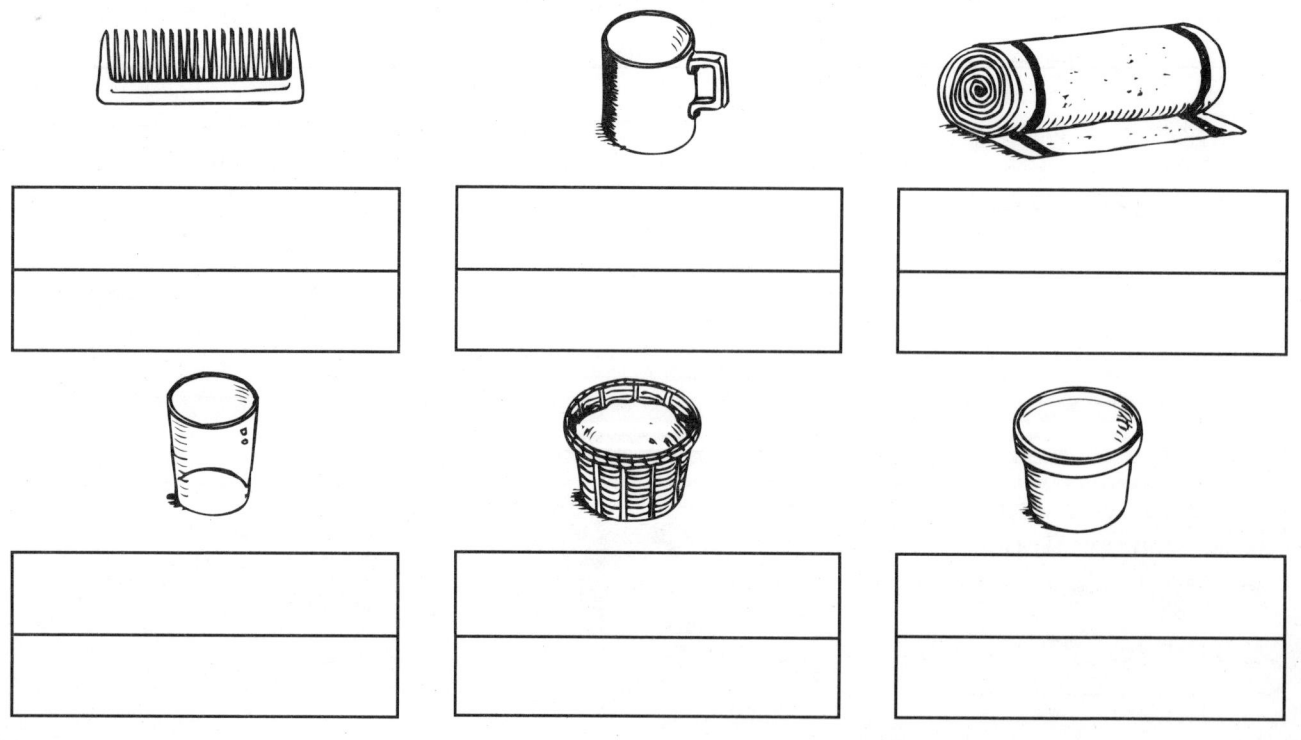

SCHOLASTIC DEVELOPING SCIENCE LANGUAGE for Materials with 8–9 year olds

Keeping warm

Keeping your body **warm** is very important. Wearing clothes helps you to do this. On a **cool** day, you can wear more clothes to stop your body losing **heat**.

Some clothes are better at keeping you warm than others. Clothes worn to keep your body warm must be made from materials that are good **thermal insulators** – that is, materials that do not allow heat to pass through them quickly.

Natural materials such as **cotton** and **wool** are good thermal insulators. Clothes made from these materials will help to keep you warm.

Air is a good thermal insulator. Warm air trapped between your body and your clothes, or between layers of clothes, helps to keep you warm.

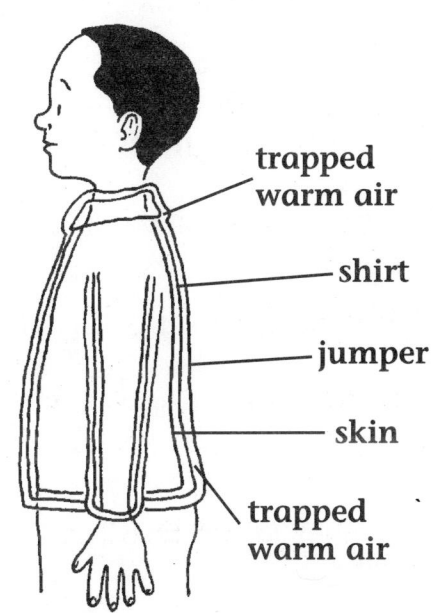

Snow is a good thermal insulator. People and animals trapped in snowdrifts are often kept alive by the **insulating properties** of the snow: it stops their bodies losing heat.

Many animals have a built-in method of keeping warm. They grow a layer of **fur**, **hair** or **feathers** to trap air and form a barrier to heat loss.

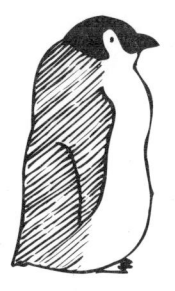 

Keeping warm

1. Why do you wear more clothes on a **cool** day?

   _____

2. Why do materials like **cotton** and **wool** help to keep you **warm**?

   _____

3. Choose the correct words from the box to complete this sentence.

   _____ , _____ , _____ and _____ are all good thermal insulators.

steel	aluminium	cotton	copper
snow	iron	air	wool

4. How do **fur**, **hair** and **feathers** help to keep many animals **warm**?

   _____

5. Tick the materials you think will be good **thermal insulators**.

   wood ☐   cardboard ☐   metal ☐   rubber ☐

6. Why does each of these objects have either a **wooden** or a **plastic** handle?

   _____

7. True or false? Underline the correct answer.
   - Thermal **insulators** get hot quickly. **True / False**
   - Thermal **conductors** get hot quickly. **True / False**

These items are all thermal insulators: a thick curtain, a table mat, a polystyrene cup, a glove. Draw labelled diagrams to show how they work. Write about how they help us.

Keeping warm

1. What do you wear to keep your body **warm**? _____

2. Fill in the missing words in these sentences.

   On a _____ day, you wear more clothes to stop your body

   losing _____.

   Some _____ are better at keeping you warm than others.

3. Name two natural clothing materials that are good **thermal insulators**.

   _____

4. True or false? Cross out the wrong answer.
   - **Air** is a good thermal insulator.   **True / False**
   - **Snow** is a very poor thermal insulator.   **True / False**

5. What body covering does each of these animals have to keep it **warm**?

   duck _____ rabbit _____ horse _____

6. Tick the **materials** you think will be good **thermal insulators**.

   | wood ☐ | glass ☐ | cardboard ☐ | aluminium ☐ |
   | steel ☐ | rubber ☐ | iron ☐ | plastic ☐ |

7. Explain how you can stop your body losing heat.

   _____

   _____

   _____

These items are all **thermal insulators**: a thick curtain, a table mat, a polystyrene cup, a glove. Choose one and draw a diagram to show how it works.

How hot is it?

Write the **temperature** that each **thermometer** shows.

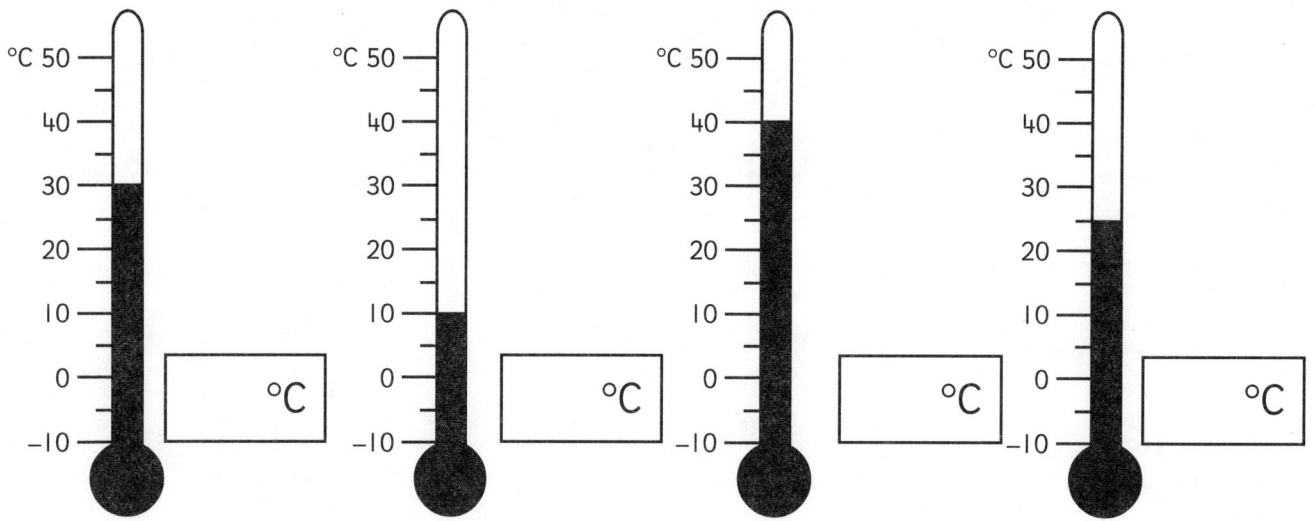

Draw on each thermometer to show the temperature.

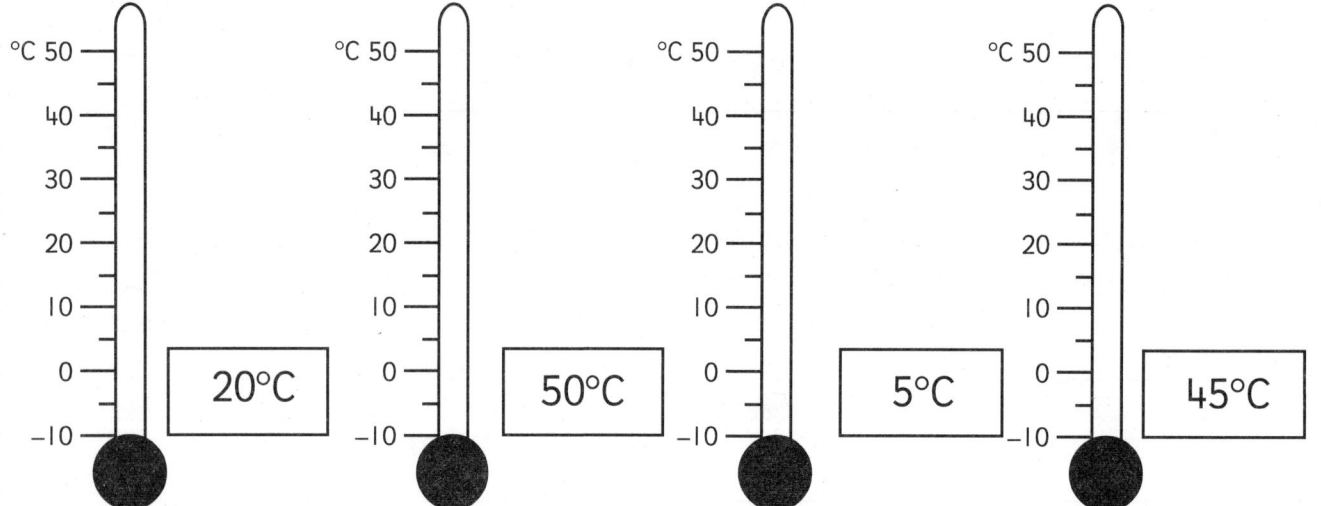

Find out the temperature at which water:

boils _____ °C   freezes _____ °C

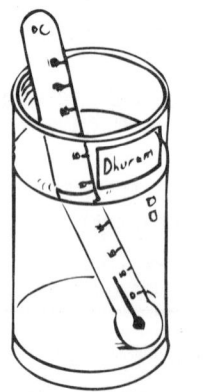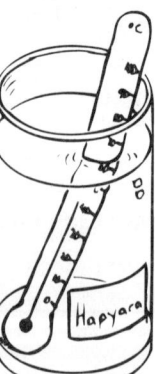

This picture shows two glasses of water. Both are in a classroom where the **room temperature** stays at 20°C.

What do you think the **temperature** of the water in each glass will be after 12 hours? No one will touch the glasses during this time.

Dhuram's glass: _____ °C   Hapyara's glass? _____ °C

Reading results

Ryan and Kelly measured the **temperature** of six samples of water. Their results are shown on this block graph.

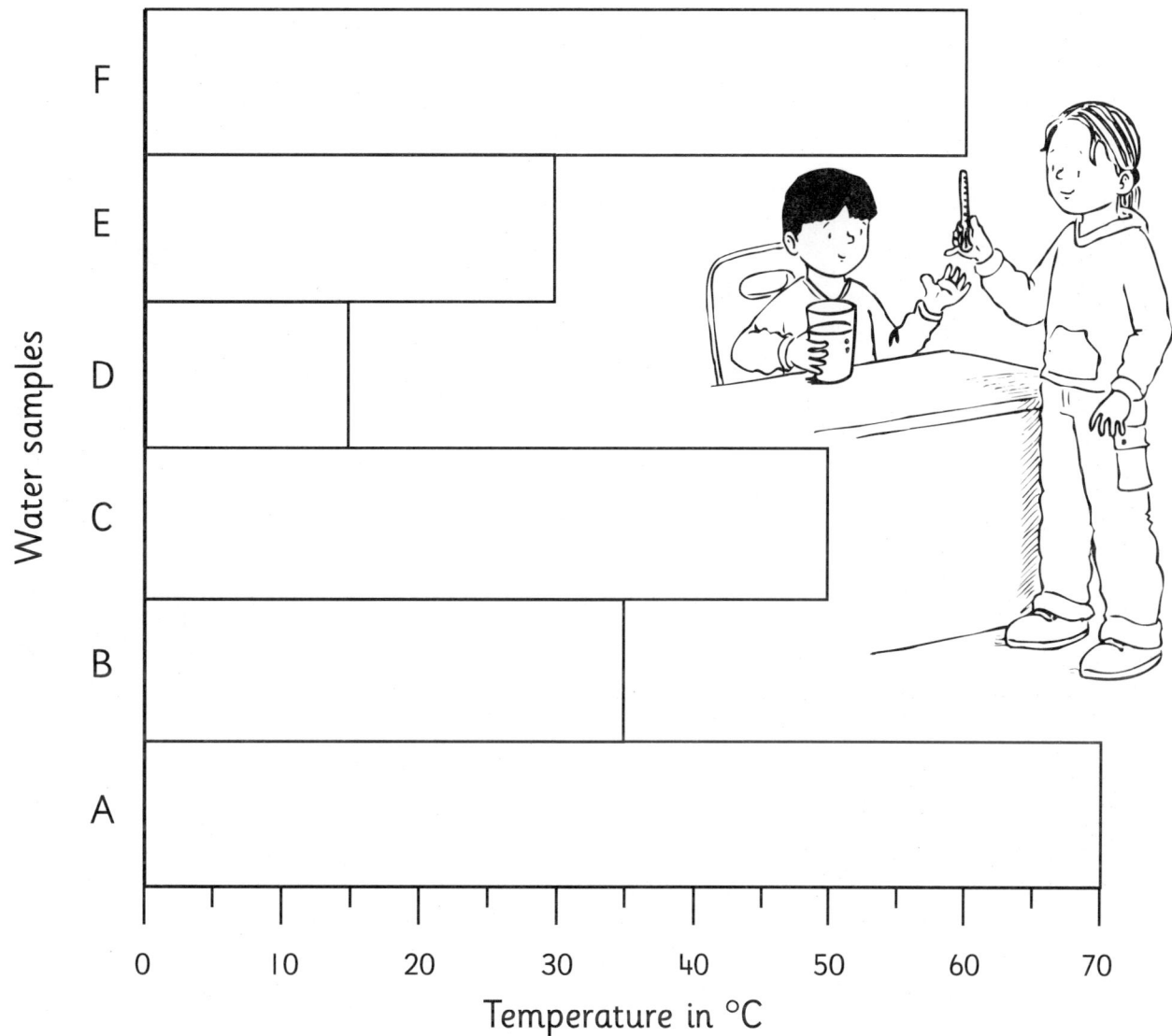

Use the information on the graph to help you answer these questions. Write your answers on another sheet of paper. Use complete sentences.

1. Which sample of water was the **warmest**?
2. Which sample of water was the **coolest**?
3. Which sample was **double** the temperature of Sample E?
4. Which sample was **half** the temperature of Sample A?
5. Which sample was **cooler** than Sample F but **warmer** than Sample B?
6. Which sample was **warmer** than Sample E but **cooler** than Sample C?

Photocopiable

Looking for differences

Katy and Stephanie measured the **temperature** of the **air** in six different areas of the classroom. Their results are shown in this plan.

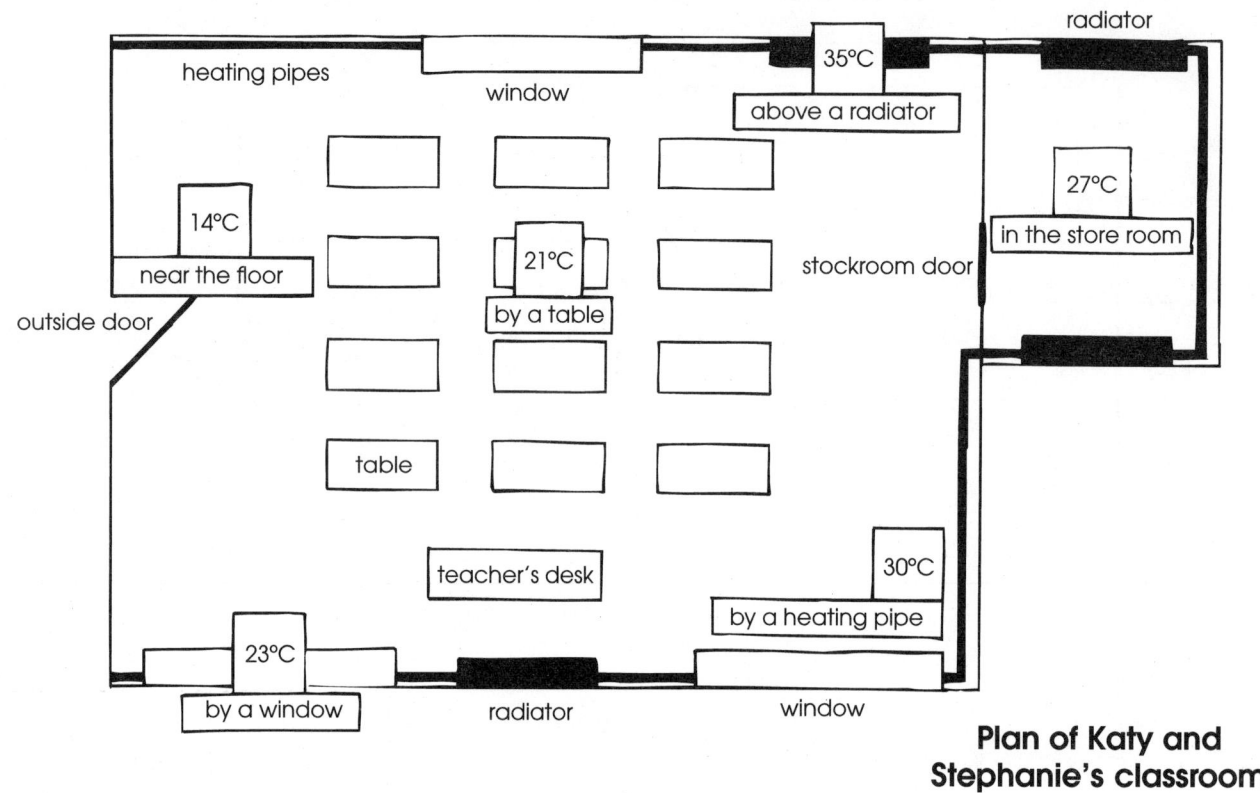

Plan of Katy and Stephanie's classroom

Use the information in the plan to help you answer these questions.

Where was the **air temperature:**

- the highest? _____

Why was the air **warmer** here than anywhere else in the room?

_____

- the lowest? _____

Why was the air **colder** here than anywhere else in the room?

_____

Why was the air **warmer** in the store room than in the middle of the classroom? _____

_____

Finding differences

You will need: the 'Looking for differences' sheet, the 'Report sheet' and a **temperature sensor** or **thermometer**.

Instructions
- Draw a plan of your classroom on the back of this sheet.
- Measure the **air temperature** in up to six different parts of the classroom.
- Write the temperatures on your plan in the way that Katy and Stephanie did.
- As you do the investigation, make notes to help you answer the questions below.

Notes

1. In how many places did you measure the air temperature?

2. On this table, write the name of each place and the temperature measurement for it.

Place name	Temp. (°C)

3. Why do you think the **warmest** place had a **higher** temperature than anywhere else?

_____

_____

_____

4. Why do you think the **coldest** place had a **lower** temperature than anywhere else?

_____

_____

Report sheet

Write a **report** on your investigation into the air temperature in your classroom. Include drawings and diagrams if necessary.

Investigation title:

Purpose of investigation:

Equipment used:

What I did:

What I found out:

Materials and electricity

An **electrical conductor** allows **electricity** to **flow** through it. An **electrical insulator** does not allow **electricity** to **flow** through it.

Liam and Nasreen tested six **materials** to find out which of them were **electrical conductors**. Here are the instructions they followed. The results they obtained are shown in the **chart**.

You will need: a 1.25v bulb and holder, a 1.5v battery (cell), Blu-tack, four wires (each about 10cm long), a **plastic** comb, a **steel** spoon, a **wooden** ruler, some **aluminium** foil, an **iron** nail, a **rubber** glove.

What to do:

1. Set up the circuit as shown in this diagram. The bulb should light.

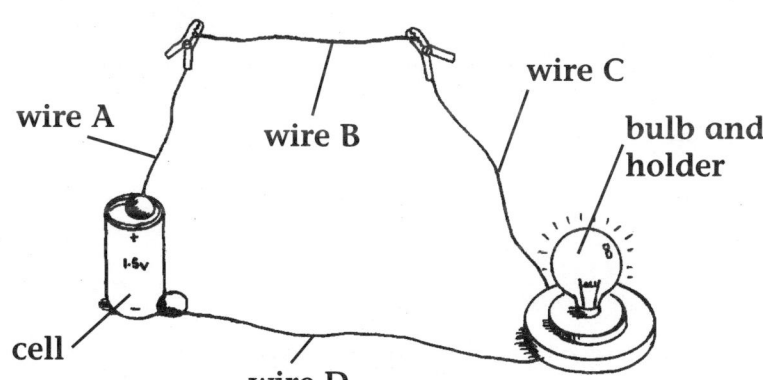

	bulb lights	bulb does not light
spoon	✓	
comb		✓
ruler		✓
foil	✓	
glove		✓
nail	✓	

2. Remove wire C from the circuit and replace it with the steel spoon. If the bulb lights up, the material the spoon is made from is an **electrical conductor**. If it does not light up, the material the spoon is made from is an **electrical insulator**.

3. Does the bulb light up? Record the result by putting a tick in the correct column on the **chart**.

4. Now test the other five **materials** in the same way. Remember to record your results on the **chart**.

Materials and electricity

1. What do we call a **material** that:

   • lets **electricity** through? _____

   • does not let **electricity** through? _____

2. Name the **materials** that Liam and Nasreen tested.

   _____

3. Shade the **materials** that are good **electrical insulators**.

| plastic | steel | wood | iron | aluminium | rubber |

4. What does it mean in the test if the bulb lights up?

   _____

   What does it mean if the bulb does not light up?

   _____

5. Name the first **material** that was tested. _____

6. Write the names of three other good **electrical conductors** that were not tested.

   _____

7. Imagine that you are testing an **electrical conductor**, but the bulb will not light up. Why not? Can you think of three possible reasons?

   a) _____

   b) _____

   c) _____

Draw an empty **chart** like the one filled in by Liam and Nasreen. Test six other materials and record the results on your chart.
Do not write the name of each **object** in the first column. Write the name of the **material** from which it is made.

Materials and electricity

1. Write the missing words in these sentences.

   An _____ **conductor** allows electricity to flow through it.

   An **electrical** _____ does not allow electricity to flow through it.

2. How many **materials** did Liam and Nasreen test? _____

   What were they? _____

3. Circle the good **electrical insulators**.

4. Four lengths of **wire** were needed in the test.
   Roughly how long did each piece of wire need to be? _____

5. Which two things were joined together by wire D?

   _____

6. What can you say about the **electrical properties** of **metals** from Liam and Nasreen's test results?

   _____

7. Why was it important to make sure that the ends of wires A and B were making a good **contact** with the materials being tested?

   _____
   _____

Draw a **chart** like the one filled in by Liam and Nasreen. Instead of writing the names of the six **objects**, write the names of the **materials** the objects were made from.
Test four other materials and add their results to your chart.

Cut and place

You will need: a copy of the 'Cut and place chart', scissors, adhesive.

Instructions:
1. Carefully cut round each picture and each label.
2. Stick each picture into the correct column on the chart.
3. Stick each label into the box below the correct picture.

rubber 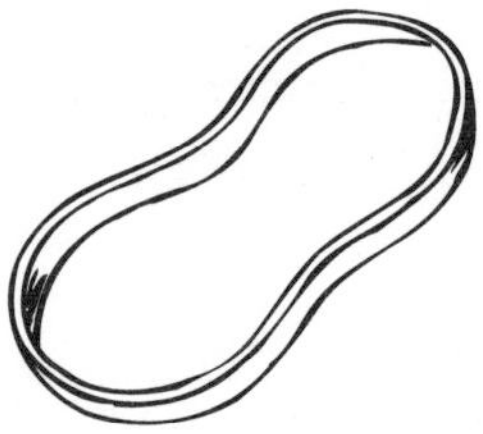	rock 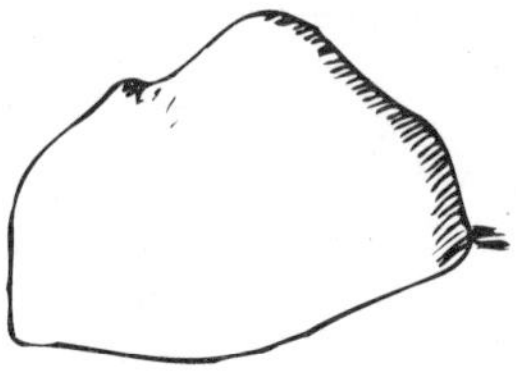	copper 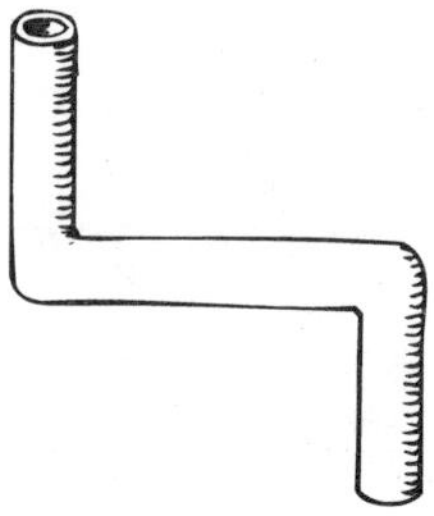
paper 	iron 	wood 
glass 	gold 	steel 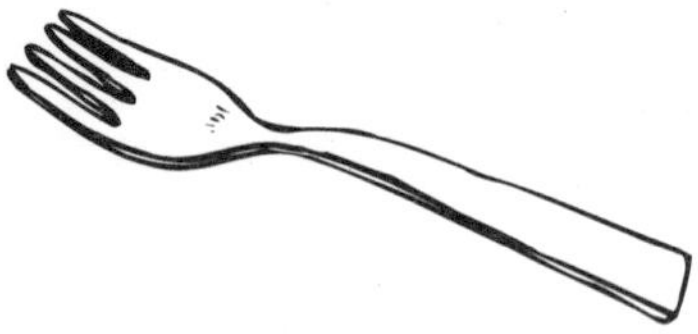
silver 	aluminium 	plastic 

Cut and place chart

Name _____ Class _____

electrical conductor	electrical insulator

Enlarge to A3 size.

Electrical facts

Choose the correct words from the box to complete these sentences.

electrical	conductors	plastic	electrical	insulators
electricity	water	metals	dry	copper
flow	wires	materials		

_____ is a form of energy that can flow through some _____ but not through others. Materials that electricity can _____ through easily are called _____ _____.

_____ are good electrical conductors. Silver and _____ are among the best. Copper, which is much cheaper than silver, is generally used for making electrical _____ and connections. Materials through which electricity cannot flow easily are called _____ _____. _____, glass, paper and most natural materials are good electrical insulators. _____ air is a good electrical insulator. Pure _____ is also a good electrical insulator. Impure water is an electrical conductor.

Write each **material** in the correct row of the table below.

tin   cork   wood   aluminium   iron   stone

| electrical conductor | |
| electrical insulator | |

Magnetic materials

Most materials are not magnetic. To be **magnetic** a material must be **attracted** by a **magnet**.

A magnet is a piece of **iron** or **steel** that has an invisible **force**. This force, called **magnetism**, makes other objects made of iron or steel **stick to** it. **Iron** and **steel** are therefore known as **magnetic materials**. As well as being attracted by a magnet, iron and steel can also be made into magnets.

Other items made out of materials such as plastic, wood, cardboard and glass will not be attracted to a magnet. This is because these materials are not **magnetic**. They are **non-magnetic** materials.

Some people think all metals are magnetic. This is not true. Metals such as copper, aluminium, tin and silver are not affected by a magnet in any way.

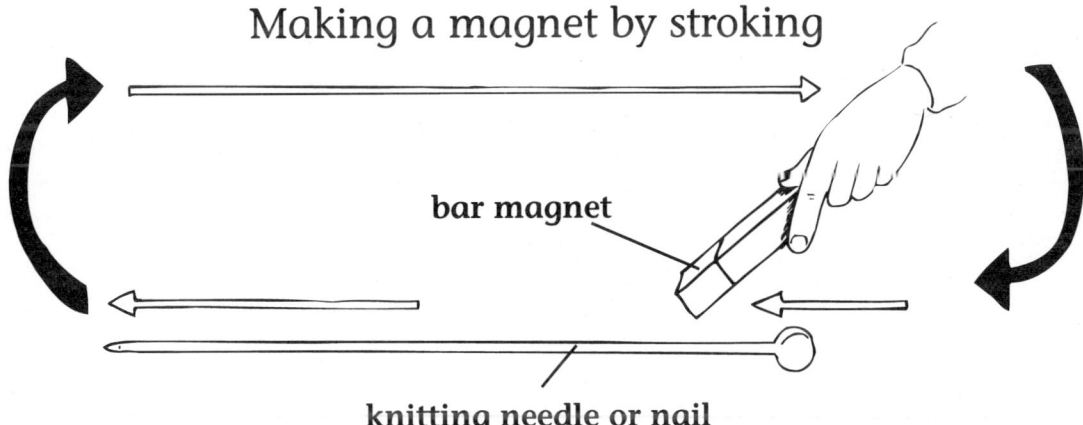

Stroke a steel nail or knitting needle with a **bar magnet** about fifty times. Move the magnet in one direction only, and raise it at the end of each stroke.

You have a new magnet! Your **magnetised** nail or needle will pick up small items made of iron or steel, such as drawing pins, staples and paper clips.

Magnetic materials

1. Fill in the missing words in these sentences.

   - To be _____, a material must be attracted by a _____.

   - _____ and _____ are magnetic materials.

   - Metals such as _____, _____, _____ and _____ are not affected by a magnet in any way.

2. A magnet has an invisible **force**. What is it called? _____

3. Name one **metal** that a **magnet** can be made from. _____

4. Name four materials that are not metals and are not magnetic.
   _____

5. Write the names of four metals that are not magnetic.
   _____

6. Which two items would you need to make a magnet? Write your answer as a complete sentence.
   _____

7. Use the boxes below to write lists of **magnetic** and **non-magnetic** items in your classroom.

Non-magnetic	

Magnetic	

Use a **magnet** to discover which objects in your classroom are made from a combination of **magnetic** and **non-magnetic** materials. Write their names and the materials they are made from.

Magnetic materials

1. True or false?
- Most materials are **magnetic**. _____
- **Iron** and **steel** are magnetic materials. _____
- **Plastic**, **wood** and **glass** are attracted by a **magnet**. _____

2. Choose the correct words from the box to complete this statement.

To be _____ a material must be _____ by a _____ .

magnet   magic   magnetic   attracted   magpie

3. A magnet has an invisible **force**. What is it called? _____

4. Which two **metals** can be made into magnets? _____

5. Find the names of some **metals** that are **not magnetic** and underline them. One has been underlined for you.

   h i s i l v e r e a d c o p p e r e p o r <u>t i n</u> i n e a l u m i n i u m a n y

6. Circle the two items that you would need to make a magnet.

   copper wire   steel nail   aluminium can   bar magnet

7. Write these items in the correct columns on the table.

Magnetic	Non-magnetic

glass bottle   bicycle frame

rubber band   iron gate

steel screw   wax crayon

Use a **magnet** to discover which objects in your classroom are made from a combination of **magnetic** and **non-magnetic** materials. Write their names and the materials they are made from.

Photocopiable

Magnetic Snap

A game for two to four players.

What to do:
- Shuffle the 'Magnetic Snap' cards and deal them out.
- All players should start with the same number of cards, face down.
- Take turns to turn over a card.
- Any player can shout **'SNAP'** if he or she sees one of the following:
  1. Two objects made of magnetic materials.
  2. A magnet and an object made of a magnetic material.
  3. Two magnets together.
- The player who shouts **'SNAP'** collects all the cards – if you all agree that player was correct. He or she starts the next round.
- The winner is the player who ends up holding all the cards.

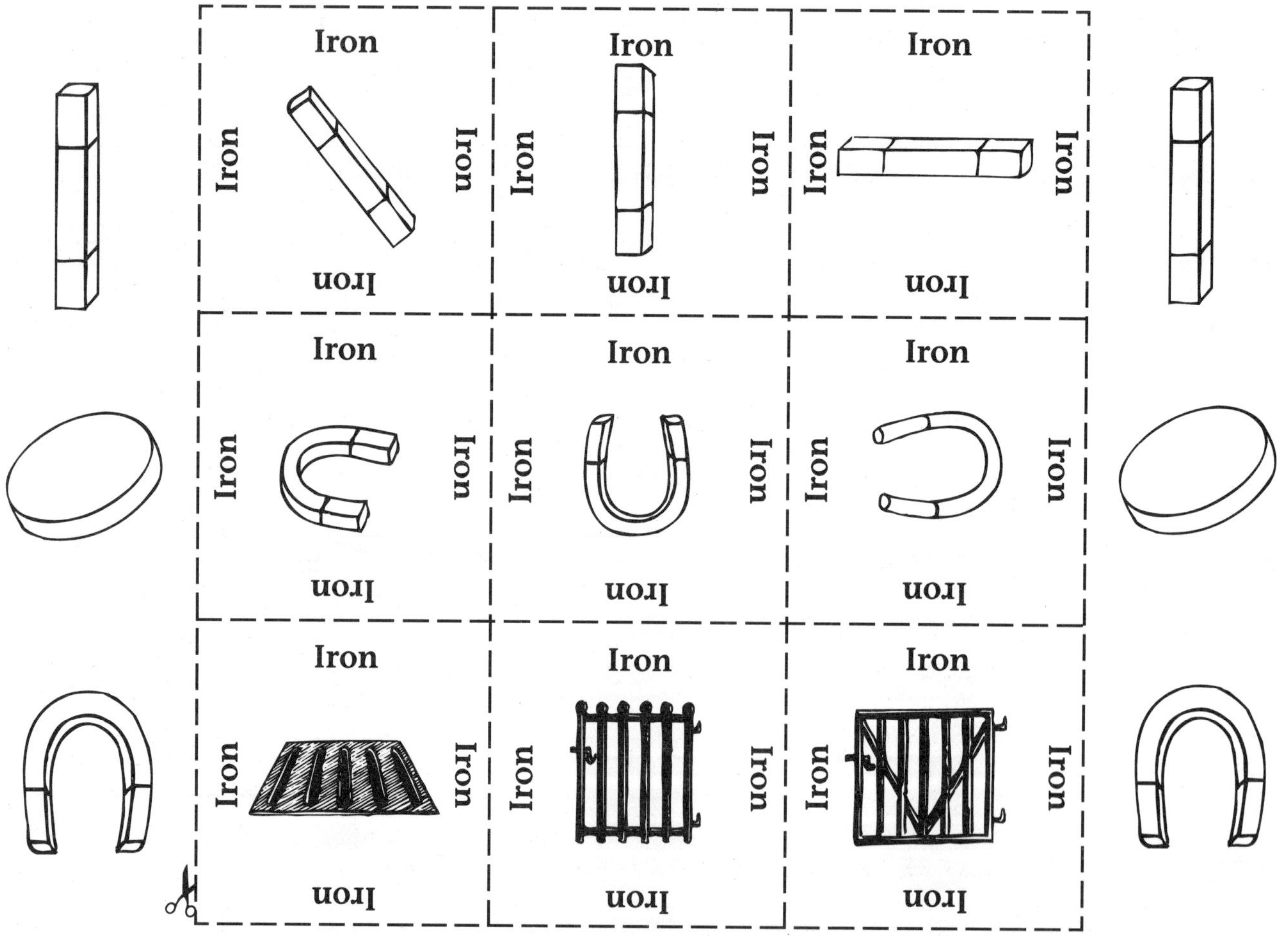

ENLARGE THE SHEETS TO A3 SIZE IF POSSIBLE.

Instructions for the teacher:
You will need two copies of this sheet, two copies of 'Magnetic Snap 2' made onto thin card, and scissors. Cut out the cards along the dotted lines. Give the cards and the set of instructions at the top of this sheet to the participating children.

Magnetic Snap

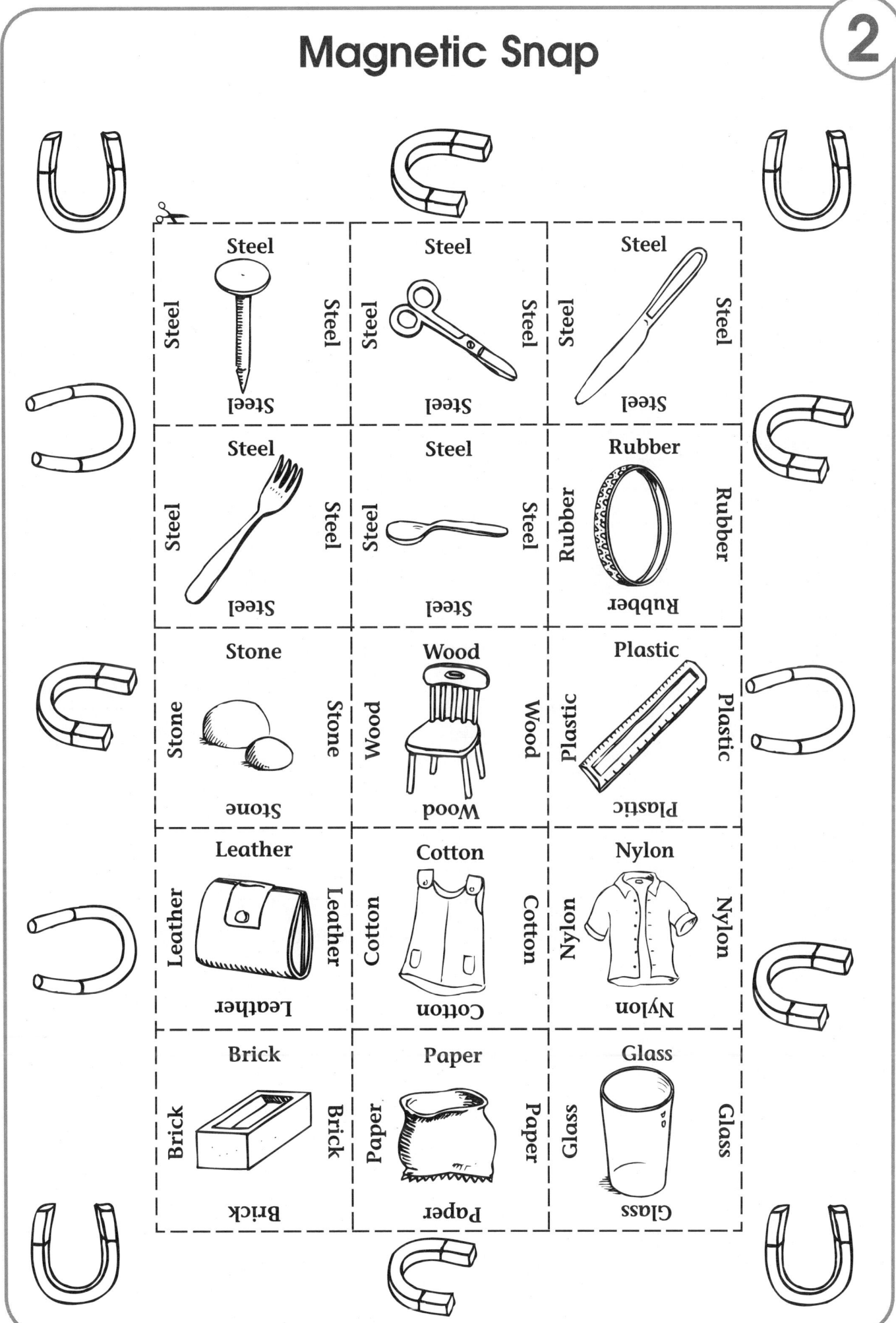

Is it attracted?

Test these objects with a **magnet** to discover which of them are either completely or partly **magnetic**. When you have tested each object, write its name in the correct place on the chart.

safety pin	ruler	aluminium foil	drawing pin	rubber band
pipe cleaner	paper clip	scissors	pencil	chalk
stapler	pencil sharpener	chair	bulldog clip	paint brush

completely or partly magnetic		completely non-magnetic	

Were all the objects with **metal** in them **magnetic**? _____

What kind of **metal** do objects have to contain to be **magnetic**?

_____

Test other classroom objects with the magnet. Try to **predict** what is going to happen before you put the magnet next to each one. Write the names of the objects that contain some **magnetic** material.

Rocks and soils

The **crust** of the Earth is made up of many different types of **rock**. The different types vary greatly in both **appearance** and **texture**.

The way **rocks** look and feel is mainly the result of how they have been formed.

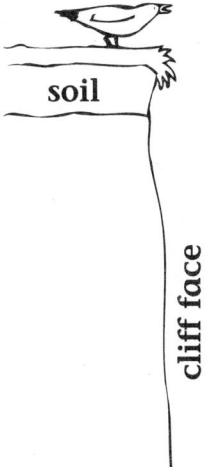

Some have been formed in layers from small pieces of rock and the remains of dead plants and animals. **Limestone** is a kind of rock made in this way. The dead plant and animal remains can often be seen as **fossils** in the rock.

Other rocks are made from rocks that have been changed by heat. **Marble** and **slate** are examples of this type of rock. Other rocks are formed when hot, liquid rock pushes itself upwards from deep inside the Earth and then cools. **Granite** is formed in this way.

All kinds of rock can occur in different sizes. We call different-sized pieces of rock by different names. For instance, very small **particles** of rock are known as **sand**; larger pieces are called **grit**, **stones** and **pebbles**; and even larger pieces are called **boulders**.

Soil makes up the outer cover of the Earth's crust. It is a mixture of very small particles of **rock**, **humus** (decaying plant and animal matter), **air spaces** and **water**.

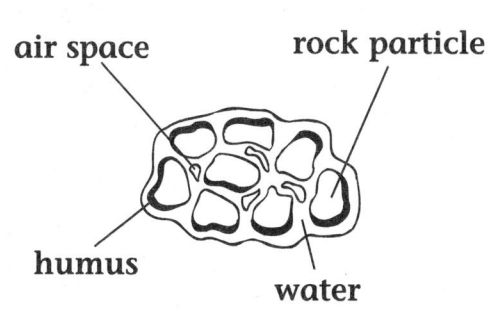

Rocks and soils

1. What is the **crust** of the Earth made of? Write a complete sentence.

   _____

2. Write two ways in which different types of **rock** can vary.

   _____

3. Describe in your own words the three main ways in which **rocks** are formed.

   • _____

   _____

   • _____

   _____

   • _____

   _____

4. Name a kind of **rock** that might contain **fossils**. _____

5. Name three kinds of rock that are each made in a different way.

   a) _____ b) _____ c) _____

6. What things is **soil** a mixture of? Give your answer as a full sentence.

   _____

   _____

7. Describe where, at the base of a cliff, the different-sized rocks are most likely to be found. Use the words **sand**, **grit**, **stones**, **pebbles** and **boulders** in your answer. Use the drawing on the text page to help you. Write your answer on the back of this sheet.

Some rocks are made from hot, liquid rock pushed up from inside the Earth. Draw and label a **volcano** to show this happening.

Rocks and soils

1. Which part of the Earth is made up of many different types of **rock**? _____

2. Write two ways in which different types of rock can vary.
   _____

3. Tick the words that are the names of different kinds of rock.

   slate ☐   granary ☐   rocket ☐

   granite ☐   limestone ☐   state ☐

4. Which kind of rock might contain **fossils**? _____

5. Circle the word that is the name for very small **particles** of rock.

   humus   sand   soil   boulders

6. Fill in the missing words.

   _____ and _____ are larger pieces of rock than **sand** but smaller than **boulders**.

7. **Soil** is a mixture of materials. Underline the names of the materials below that are most likely to be found in a sample of **soil**.

   roots   humus   small   particles of rock
   rabbits   water   humans   air

8. Find out and write the meaning of each word.

   ● appearance _____

   ● texture _____

Some rocks are made from hot, liquid rock pushed up from inside the Earth. Draw and label a **volcano** to show this happening.

Looking at rocks

You will need: five samples of different kinds of rock labelled A to E, a hand lens, an eye dropper, water, a steel nail, paper, pens, card.

What to do:

1. Look carefully at each sample of rock.
Record its **shape** and **texture** with a tick (✓) in the correct columns on the chart, then write its colour.

Sample	Shape			Texture		Colour
	round	flat	jagged	rough	smooth	
A						
B						
C						
D						
E						

2. Use the dropper to place **one** droplet of water on the **surface** of each sample. Leave for **one** minute.
Has the water **soaked** into the rock? Write either **Yes** or **No** in the table below. If the water has soaked in, then the rock is **permeable**.

	Permeable or not?				
rock	A	B	C	D	E
result					

3. **Scratch** each rock with the point of a steel nail. Does it scratch easily?
Write the letters of the rocks in order of **hardness** in this table.

	Order of hardness				
softest						hardest

4. Choose **one** of the rock samples and make a display label for it. Use your experiments to help you. Remember to mention its texture, whether it is permeable and how hard it is.

5. With your friends, make a display of the rocks and your labels.

Hidden rocks

In this wordsearch there are twelve names of different kinds of rock. Some letters for these names are given as clues below.
Find the names in the grid and fill in the missing letters. The names are written in all directions except diagonally.
Draw a line through each name in the wordsearch when you find it.

c _ _ l _   m _ r _ _ _   s _ o _ _

c _ _ y   p _ _ b _ _   s _ _ d

s _ n _ _ _ o _ _   g _ _ n _ t _   b _ _ l _ e _

l _ _ _ s _ _ n _   s l _ _ e   g r _ _ l

e	n	o	t	s	d	n	a	s
n	q	c	h	a	l	k	j	e
o	g	r	a	n	i	t	e	a
t	g	d	i	d	b	f	l	p
s	r	e	d	l	u	o	b	e
e	a	t	h	n	g	k	r	b
m	v	a	y	a	l	c	a	b
i	e	l	c	m	o	l	m	l
l	l	s	p	s	t	o	n	e

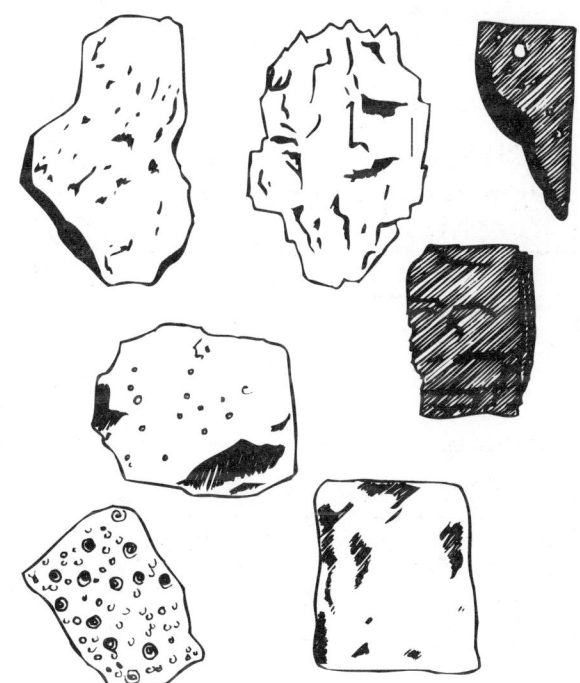

Use reference books or a CD-ROM to find the names of some other kinds of rock not included in the wordsearch. Write them in this box.

DEVELOPING SCIENCE LANGUAGE for Materials with 8–9 year olds   SCHOLASTIC

Facts about soil

Draw a line to join the first half of each sentence to the correct ending.

Different kinds of soil	easily dug.
Humus consists	plants and darkness for germinating seeds.
Soil gives cover for young	easily waterlogged.
Plant roots take in water	have different properties.
Clay soils are sticky	contain many air spaces.
The water in soil contains dissolved	particles in soil are filled with either air or water.
The spaces between the solid	covering of the Earth's crust.
Clay soils are	and hard to dig.
Soil is a	minerals that are needed by plants.
Sandy soils are loose and	of rotting plant and animal remains.
Soil makes up the outer	from the soil.
Sandy soils drain easily and	mixture of sand, clay, humus, minerals, water and air.

What is soil made of?

Adam and Kyle wanted to **separate** the different **materials** found in **soil**. They mixed a sample of soil with water in a clear container and left it to stand for a few days. The drawing below shows what the mixture looked like then. Choose the correct name to write for each label.

clay

humus

water

gravel

sand

Adam and Kyle want to sort out the different-sized particles from a dry sample of this soil. How could they use two sieves with different-sized holes to do this? Draw a **diagram** to help you explain.

Down to Earth clues

Work with a friend to solve the clues.
You will both need a copy of this sheet and a pencil.
Ask your teacher what you have to do.

Set A clues

1. Goes hard when baked.
2. Plants grow in this.
3. Rock made of sand.
4. Beach castles can be made of this.
5. Rock often carved and polished into statues.
6. Grass-covered ground.
7. Collection of small stones.
8. Rock used as a roofing material.

Set B clues

1. Soft, white rock used for writing on a blackboard.
2. Small, rounded stone.
3. Decaying plant and animal remains.
4. Makes soil moist.
5. This hard rock is called _ r _ n _ t _.
6. Large, rounded stone.
7. Dead remains preserved in rock.
8. Whitish rock often containing fossils.

Word list

pebble   sand   limestone   turf   slate   granite   water   clay
fossil   sandstone   gravel   chalk   soil   marble   boulder   humus

Answers

1.	5.
2.	6.
3.	7.
4.	8.

COVER THESE INSTRUCTIONS WHEN PHOTOCOPYING.

Instructions for the teacher:
The children work in pairs. Agree who will read out each set of clues.
The child who reads the Set A clues must try to find the most suitable answers from the word list to the Set B clues. The child who reads the Set B clues must try to find the most suitable answers from the word list to the Set A clues. Each answer should be written carefully in the correct answer box.

Types of change

Materials are **changing** all the time.

Some of these **changes** in materials can be undone. The material can be changed back to how it was. Most changes of this kind are caused by a change in **temperature**.

A change in **temperature** can alter the way a material looks. For example, a **rise** in temperature can make a **solid** change into a **liquid**. A **fall** in temperature can make a **liquid** change into a **solid**.
These changes are the result of **processes** called **melting** and **freezing**. For example, a rise in temperature can make solid **ice melt** to liquid **water**. A fall in temperature can make **water freeze** to **ice**.

A rise in temperature will cause chocolate or wax to melt from a solid into a liquid. If the temperature then falls, these materials will become solid again.

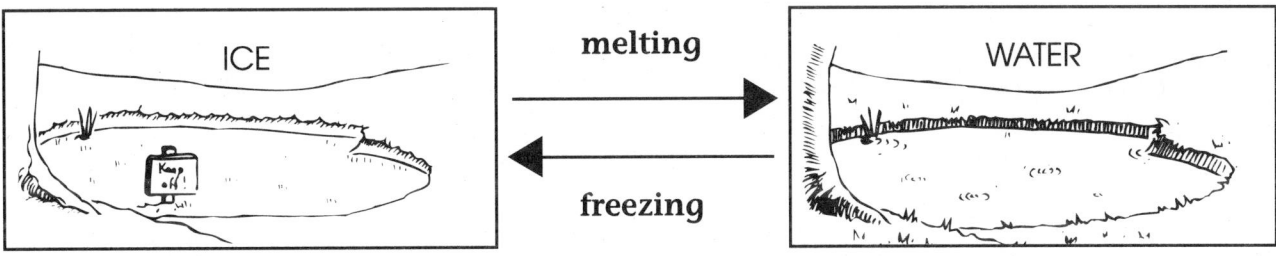

Some changes to materials cannot be undone. The material cannot be changed back into how it was, because a different material has been formed.

Burning is an example of a change to a material after which the material cannot be changed back to how it was.

Types of change

1. Do materials always stay the same? Answer 'Yes' or 'No'. _____

2. What causes most **changes** in materials that can be undone?
   _____

   In what way can a **change** in **temperature** alter a material?
   _____
   _____

3. Give the name of each **process**.

   a) A solid changing into a liquid. _____

   b) A liquid changing into a solid. _____

4. Complete this sentence.
   A **rise** in **temperature** will cause chocolate or wax to _____
   _____

5. What has been formed when the change to a material cannot be undone? _____

6. Name three materials not mentioned in the text that will **melt** in bright summer sunlight. _____

7. The way water looks can be altered by a change in **temperature**. Circle the materials below that are forms of water.

   snow   rock   hail   oil   ice

   lightning   frost   sleet   soil   rain

On another sheet of paper, draw and name three things people do that result in a change to a material that can be undone. Then draw and name three things people do that result in a change to a material that cannot be undone.

Types of change

1. Do materials always stay the same? Write 'Yes' or 'No'. _____

2. Write in the missing words in these sentences.
a) Most **changes** that can be undone are caused by a **change** in _____.

b) A **change** in **temperature** can alter the way a material _____.

3. True or false? Cross out the wrong answer.
a) A material that is **melting** is changing from a solid to a liquid.
True / False

b) A material that is **freezing** is changing from a solid to a liquid.
True / False

4. Complete these sentences, using one word each time.

a) When ice **melts** it changes into _____.

b) When water **freezes** it changes into _____.

5. Cross out the incorrect words in this sentence.

When a material **burns / melts / freezes**, it cannot then be changed back into how it was.

6. Name three materials not mentioned in the text that will **melt** in bright, summer sunlight. _____

7. The way water looks can be altered by a change in **temperature**. Circle the materials below that are forms of water.

snow   rock   hail   oil   ice

When a cake mixture is baked, a change takes place that cannot be undone. What other things do people do that result in a change to a material that cannot be undone? Write and draw pictures on another sheet of paper.

What will happen?

Kanthar and Milesh wanted to find out whether any changes occurred when these solids were mixed with water:

sand, salt, chalk, sugar, flour, sawdust.

They filled six clear containers with water. Into each container they stirred a tablespoonful of a solid for 10 seconds. They left each mixture to stand for 15 minutes.

Draw what you think each mixture will look like after that length of time. The sand has been drawn for you.

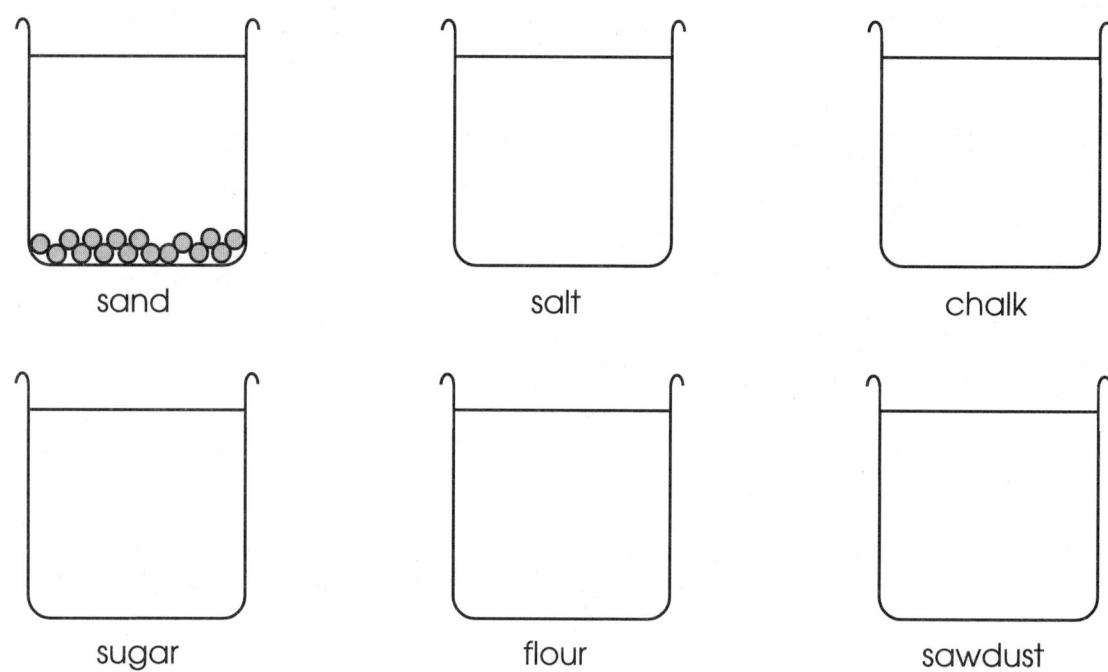

Briefly write on the table what happened to each material.

sand	stayed the same, sank	sugar	
salt		flour	
chalk		sawdust	

Notes for the teacher:
COVER THESE INSTRUCTIONS WHEN PHOTOCOPYING.
The children can fill in this sheet either by using their own knowledge (making predictions throughout) or by making predictions and then carrying out the experiments.

Changes

The change in a material when it **melts, freezes, boils, dissolves, evaporates** or **condenses** can be undone. No new **substance** has been formed.

The change in a material when it **burns** or **rusts** cannot be undone. A new **substance** has been created which is different from the original material.

1. Write the missing word in each of these sentences.

- No new _____ is formed when a material **melts, freezes, boils, dissolves, evaporates** or **condenses**.

- A new **substance** is formed when a material _____ or _____.

2. **Cross** the changes where no new **substance** is formed. **Tick** the changes where a new **substance** is formed.

butter melting	☐	plaster of Paris hardening	☐
salt dissolving	☐	a candle burning	☐
bread baking	☐	water evaporating	☐

3. Rearrange each of these groups of letters into the name of a kind of change where no new **substance** is formed. The first letter of each word has been written as a capital letter. The pictures give you clues.

lMet   trEapvaoe   erFeze

eCnodens   vsDisole   oiBl

Changing shape

This crossword puzzle has ten words. Each word is a different way of changing the shape of something.
Write a suitable clue for each word. Use a dictionary to help you. The first clue has been written for you.

Clues Across

1. To force something into a curve or angle.

5. _____

6. _____

9. _____

```
 1B  2E  N   D
     X              3S      4C
  5P  R  E  S  S    Q       U
     A              U       R
     N          6S  W  E  L  L
     D              E
              7W    Z       8F
              A     E       L
          9C  R  U  S  H    E
              P     H       X
```

Clues Down

2. _____

3. _____

4. _____

6. _____

7. _____

8. _____

Heating and cooling

A change in **temperature** takes place if a material is either **heated** or **cooled**.

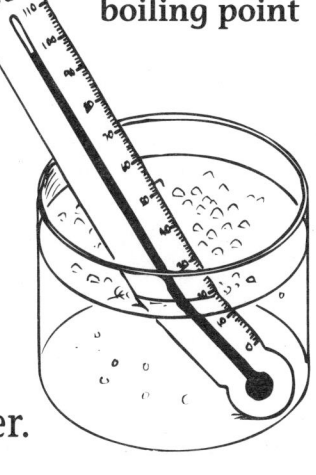
boiling point

A **rise** in temperature can cause a material to **expand** slightly. This means that it gets bigger.

A **fall** in temperature can cause a material to **contract** slightly. This means that it gets smaller.

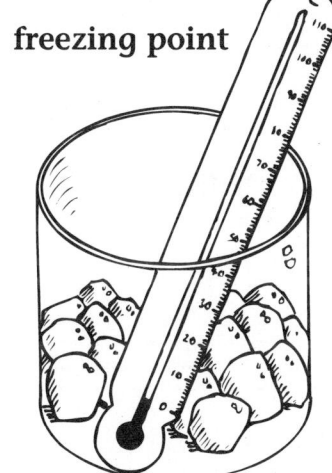
freezing point

If we want to know the temperature of something, we measure it using a **thermometer**.

A thermometer has a temperature **scale** measured in **degrees Celsius** (°C). Each mark on the scale usually measures one **degree** of temperature. The marks on a thermometer usually range from 0°C (the **freezing point** of water) to 100°C (the **boiling point** of water).

The way a material looks may change when it is either **heated** or **cooled**.

A **rise** in temperature can change a **solid** into a **liquid**. This happens to chocolate when it is heated. It **melts**.

A **fall** in temperature can change a **liquid** into a **solid**. This happens to water when it is cooled to 0°C. It **freezes**.

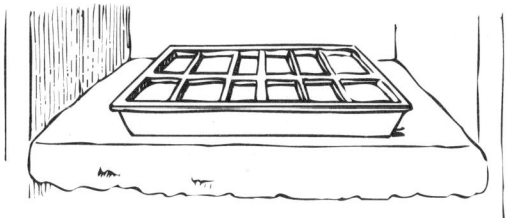

Heating and cooling

1. What must happen to a material for its **temperature** to change?
   _____

2. What must happen to a material for it to:

a) expand? _____

b) contract? _____

3. What instrument is used to find the **temperature** of something? Write your answer as a sentence.
   _____

4. Which **temperature scale** is most commonly used in **thermometers**?
   _____

5. At what **temperature** does water: **a)** boil? ____ °C **b)** freeze? ____°C

6. What may happen to a **solid** when its **temperature** rises?
   _____

7. Describe what happens to chocolate when it is heated. Draw and label a diagram to go with your writing.

   _____
   _____
   _____
   _____
   _____

Draw a series of labelled diagrams to show what happens to butter and wax when they are heated.
Use reference books or CD-ROMs to find the names of some other materials that melt easily when heated.

Heating and cooling

1. Choose the correct words from the box to complete this sentence.

   A change in _____ takes place if a material is

   either _____ or _____.

   | change   cooled   temperature   material   heated |

2. Cross out the incorrect words in these sentences.
   a) A **rise / fall** in **temperature** can cause a material to **expand**.
   b) A **rise / fall** in **temperature** can cause a material to **contract**.

3. What is the name of this instrument?

   _____

4. Circle the word that is the name of a **temperature scale**.

   MATERIAL   THERMOMETER   DEGREES   CELSIUS   TEMPERATURE

5. At what **temperature** does water: a) boil?___ °C b) freeze? ___°C

6. What happens to:

   a) chocolate when it is **heated**? _____

   b) water when it is **cooled** to 0°C? _____

7. Write 'True' or 'False' after this statement.
   An ice-lolly will **melt** if the surrounding air **temperature** is above 0°C.

   _____

Draw a series of labelled diagrams to show what happens to butter and wax when they are heated.
Can you think of any other materials that melt easily when heated?

What will happen if...?

Describe what happens to each of these materials when it is heated. The first one has been done for you.

Material	Appearance while being heated	Description of what happens
WATER		The water was still and clear. Then bubbles started to form on the bottom and float up. Steam started to rise and the water began to shake.
MILK		
CANDLE WAX		
CHOCOLATE		
CAKE MIXTURE		
CLAY		

COVER THESE INSTRUCTIONS WHEN PHOTOCOPYING.

Notes for the teacher:
The children can fill in this sheet either by using their own knowledge or by carrying out the experiments **under strict adult supervision.** All of these experiments are potentially hazardous.

Expansion and contraction

The words in capital letters are in the wrong sentences. Sort them out and write the most suitable word opposite each sentence number in the box on the right. The first one has been done for you.

1. Materials **HEATED** when they are heated.
2. Materials **FREEZES** when they are cooled.
3. When **STEEL**, liquids expand much more than solids.
4. Heated **THERMOMETERS** expand much less than liquids.
5. When water **CONTRACT** it expands.
6. Liquids which expand rapidly when heated, such as alcohol and mercury, are used in **SOLIDS**.
7. Metals such as ~~**EXPAND**~~ expand and contract more easily than most other solids.

1.	EXPAND
2.	
3.	
4.	
5.	
6.	
7.	

Discuss and then write down why you think plastic rain gutters and downpipes 'creak' when the Sun shines on them.

_____

_____

Discuss and then write down why you think central heating radiators 'creak' as they cool down.

_____

_____

COVER THESE INSTRUCTIONS WHEN PHOTOCOPYING.

Notes for the teacher:
The children can fill in this sheet either by using their knowledge or by carrying out the experiments **under adult supervision**. All of these experiments are potentially hazardous.

Temperature squares

This is a word building game.

Start at a shaded square. Move on to a square touching the letter you are on. The next square can be in any direction, including a diagonal.

Keep moving on until you have made one of the ten words in the box on the right. The shaded square will contain the first letter. Shade in, cross out or connect up the other letters as you build the word.

Make all ten of the words in the box. Not all the letters in the grid will be used. One of the words has been made for you.

t	e	j	m	r	a	k	q	b	i
v	m	a	t	u	w	g	i	l	o
p	o	r	c	n	y	n	g	e	
j	o	o	e	z	i	k	q	p	x
l	f	v	y	e	c	n	j	d	a
q	u	r	e	v	t	o	y	n	h
c	g	n	t	s	a	c	t	j	o
o	k	i	f	l	e	m	e	t	t
l	d	q	r	v	t	s	y	j	k
e	s	v	y	o	m	o	m	q	j
j	t	y	z	e	v	q	r	h	k
q	k	n	e	t	e	r	e	v	t

freezing
~~temperature~~
warm
cool
boiling
hottest
coldest
thermometer
melting
frozen

Write down any other words you can think of to do with temperature. Next to each word, write down what it means.

_____

_____

_____

_____

Soluble or insoluble?

Charlotte and Mundeep tested some **materials**. They knew that materials that **dissolve** in water are called **soluble** and materials that do not are called **insoluble**. Now they wanted to find out which materials are **soluble** and which are **insoluble** in water.

To begin with, they gathered together all the things they needed: four jars, a teaspoon, enough water to fill the four jars; enough salt, sawdust, sugar and sand for a level teaspoon of each.

They filled a jar nearly to the top with water and put one level teaspoon of salt into the water. They stirred the salt and water slowly 50 times, then looked to see what had happened to the **mixture**. They recorded what they saw in the table. They left the mixture to stand for one hour, then looked at it and recorded what they saw in the table.

They did the same **experiment** three more times: once with sawdust, once with sugar and once with sand.

Here are their results:

Material	Appearance after mixing	Appearance after one hour
salt	slightly cloudy looking but no solid particles to be seen	clear but with a few salt particles at the bottom of the water
sawdust	particles floating about in the mixture and gradually rising	clear water with all the bits of wood floating on the surface
sugar	clear water with really nothing else to see	water looks like tap water with no particles of anything anywhere
sand	particles spinning around and around and gradually falling	water clear with all the sand at the bottom

Photocopiable

Soluble or insoluble?

1. What is the difference between a **soluble** and an **insoluble** material?
___
___

2. Which materials did Charlotte and Mundeep test for **solubility**?
___

3. Describe briefly how the test was carried out.
___
___
___
___

4. Which materials **dissolved** in this experiment?
___

5. Why were there still **salt** particles at the bottom of the salt and water mixture after an hour?
___

6. Why were particles of **sand** spinning around and around in the water immediately after mixing? ___

7. Which mixture had clear water just after mixing and also an hour later? ___

8. Write a sentence to explain how **sea water** is different from **fresh water**.
___

On the back of this sheet, write each of these words in a separate sentence to show what it means.

    mixture   soluble   insoluble   dissolved   solution

Soluble or insoluble?

1. Cross out the incorrect word.

   Insoluble / Soluble materials dissolve in water.

2. Which four materials did Charlotte and Mundeep test?

   _____

3. What did they use to **measure** how much of each material to put in each jar of water? _____

4. How long did they leave each mixture to stand before looking at it a second time? _____

5. Describe the **appearance** of the mixture of sawdust and water immediately after stirring. _____

   _____

6. Show how the mixtures with the **salt, sawdust** and **sand** in them looked after an hour.

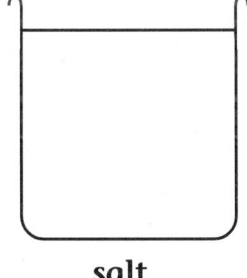
salt

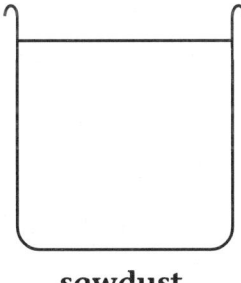
sawdust

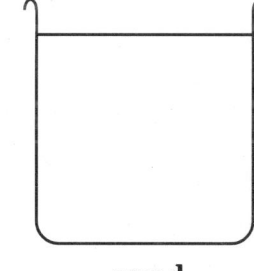
sand

7. Which materials **dissolved** in this experiment? Write your answer as a complete sentence.

   _____

   _____

Find the meanings of these words and write them on the back of this sheet.

    soluble   insoluble   dissolve   solution

DEVELOPING SCIENCE LANGUAGE for Materials with 8–9 year olds   ■ SCHOLASTIC

Missing words

Read this passage. Write in the correct missing words from the box at the bottom of the page.

A special kind of mixture

A mixture is _____ or more different things combined.

When a liquid and a solid are mixed, the _____ may break up into tiny pieces that are so small they cannot be seen with the naked eye. This happens to _____ when it is mixed with water. It also happens to sugar. Both salt and sugar break up in water into tiny _____ that cannot be seen.

Salt and sugar can both _____ in water because they are soluble. These mixtures are called _____. The mixture of salt and water is called a salt solution and the mixture with _____ in it is called a sugar solution.

Some materials do not dissolve in _____. They are insoluble. Wood, _____ and clay, for example, are insoluble. They will not dissolve in water to make a solution.

Salt or sugar can be separated from a solution by _____ the mixture so that the water evaporates and the salt or sugar is left behind.

particles	water	two	solutions	boiling
salt	solid	chalk	sugar	dissolve

Definitions

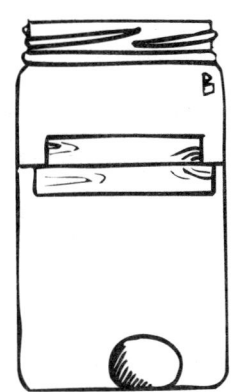

Use a **dictionary** to help you with these words.

Draw a line to join each word to its meaning. One has been done for you.

float		to drop down through air or a liquid
solvent		to be held up by air or a liquid
mixture		the dissolved part of a solution
sink		can be dissolved
soluble		a liquid into which something dissolves
solute		two or more things combined

Write the correct word or meaning in each empty box.

particle	
	mix with a liquid to make a solution
separate	
	cannot be dissolved
substance	
	a liquid containing a dissolved substance

Dissolving times

You will need: one small container made of clear plastic, a tablespoon, a dish, a teaspoon, paper, a pencil; a beaker of water, a few spoonfuls of sugar, a few spoonfuls of salt.

What to do:
1. Fill the container nearly to the top with water.
2. Slowly stir one level teaspoon of sugar into the water. Count how many stirs it takes for the sugar to **dissolve** completely.
3. Write the number of stirs in column **A** of the table. Empty the container.

Material	A (normal) Number of stirs	B (crushed) Number of stirs
sugar		
salt		

4. Now put a level teaspoon of sugar into the dish.
5. Crush the sugar to a fine powder with the back of the tablespoon.
6. Fill the container with fresh water. Slowly stir the crushed sugar into this water. Count how many stirs it takes for the sugar to **dissolve** completely.
7. Write the number of stirs in column **B** on the table. Empty the container. Answer these questions on another sheet of paper.

a) Which sugar particles **dissolved** more quickly:

the normal or the crushed? _____

b) Why do you think this was? _____

_____

8. Now do the same experiment with the salt. Write your results in the table, then answer these questions on another sheet of paper. Try to **explain** your results, not just **describe** them.
a) Which salt particles **dissolved** more quickly?
b) Is this what you expected to happen? Why?

9. Which do you think would **dissolve** faster: a sugar lump or the same mass of sugar in small grains? **Predict** the result, then try it to check.

Separating mixtures

This sheet describes two ways of **separating mixtures** of things.

SEPARATING SOLIDS BY SIZE

You will need: a mixture of sand and pebbles, a large bucket, a large sieve.

What to do:
1. Place the **sieve** on top of the bucket.
2. Pour the **mixture** of sand and pebbles into the sieve.
3. Gently shake the sieve.

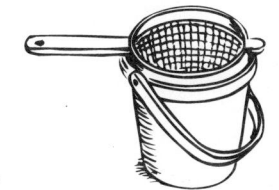

1.   2.   3.

The two solids are now **separate** from each other. The **pebbles** are in the sieve and the smaller **sand** particles are in the bucket.

SEPARATING SOLIDS FROM LIQUIDS

You will need: a mixture of sand and water, a plastic bottle, a funnel, a large piece of filter paper.

What to do:
1. Place the **funnel** in the neck of the bottle.
2. Line the inside of the funnel with a folded piece of **filter paper**.
3. Pour the sand and water mixture into the funnel.

1.   2.   3.

The liquid and solid are now **separate** from each other. The water is in the bottle and the sand is on the filter paper.

Separating mixtures

1. What does the text on the sheet describe?

   _____

2. Which two materials are being separated in **a)** the first activity and **b)** the second activity on the sheet?

   a) _____

   b) _____

3. In the first activity, which material is trapped in the **sieve**?

   _____

4. Draw a series of three labelled diagrams to show how you would separate a mixture of sand and water.

1.	2.	3.

5. In the first activity, which material is **not** trapped by the sieve? _____

6. Why does the **sieve** holding the mixture of sand and pebbles have to be gently **shaken** during the separating process?

   _____

7. Why can **filter paper** be used to **separate** solids from liquids? _____

   _____

On another sheet of paper, describe in your own words how you could separate a mixture of flour and currants. Draw labelled diagrams to go with your description.

Separating mixtures

1. Which two materials were being separated in the first activity on the sheet? _____

2. Name the **equipment** needed to **separate** a mixture of sand and water. _____

3. In the first activity, why do the pebbles not fall into the bucket?
_____

4. On another sheet of paper, draw three labelled diagrams to show how you would separate a mixture of sand and pebbles.

5. Here are the **instructions** for separating a mixture of sand and water. Number them 1, 2 and 3 in the correct order.

   ☐ Pour the sand and water mixture into the funnel.
   ☐ Place the funnel in the neck of the bottle.
   ☐ Line the inside of the funnel with filter paper.

6. Write the names of these objects under the pictures.

_____ _____ _____ _____

7. Why does the **sieve** holding the mixture of sand and pebbles need to be gently **shaken** during the separating process?
_____

Pierre, a famous French chef, has dropped a bag of currants into a bowl of flour by mistake. He has used a **bowl** and a **sieve** to separate them.
On another sheet of paper, draw a labelled diagram to show how Pierre has sorted the mixture.

Sorting solids by size

A mixture of different-sized solid particles can be sorted with a **sieve**. A sieve is a container with very small holes or a wire net in the bottom. Small solid particles pass through. Large solid particles are trapped and stay in the sieve.

1. Circle the **sieve**.

 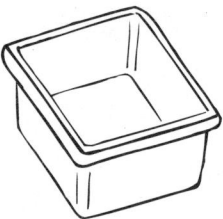  

2. Connect this sentence starter to the correct ending.

                         all solid particles pass through.

A sieve lets   **large** solid particles pass through.

                         small solid particles pass through.

3. Complete these sentences by writing in the correct words from the box below.

a) A sieve will _____ a mixture of solids of _____ sizes.

b) _____ can use _____ to separate unwanted stones from soil.

| different | sieves | gardeners | separate |

4. Draw a labelled diagram to show a **sieve** being used.

Filtering

When solids do not **dissolve** in water, they can be separated from the water by **filtering**. This is because **filter paper** is **porous**: it will let water through, but not solid particles.

When water is poured onto a piece of folded filter paper fitted in a **funnel**, the paper traps the solids but lets the water pass through.

1. Write the meaning of the word **porous**.

_____

2. Tick the materials that are **porous**.

| paper towel | ☐ | cotton cloth | ☐ | polythene sheet | ☐ |
| blotting paper | ☐ | glass window | ☐ | gauze bandage | ☐ |

3. Use writing, diagrams or both to give instructions telling someone how to filter a stirred-up mixture of water and clay using a plastic bottle, a funnel and some filter paper.
Try to use the words in the word bank below.
Jot down your ideas here, then redraft your set of instructions on another sheet of paper.

Word bank
porous
filter
clay
mixture
funnel
bottle
solid
liquid
separate

Separating questions

1. Solid particles of different sizes can be **separated** with a **sieve**. What is a **sieve**?

   _____

   _____

2. **Undissolved** solids can be **separated** from a liquid using a sheet of **filter paper**. What is **filter paper**?

   _____

   _____

3. **Dissolved** solids can be **separated** from a liquid by **evaporating** the liquid. What does **evaporating** mean?

   _____

   _____

4. What method would you use to separate each of these mixtures? Choose one word from the box on the right.

   a) small stones and soil _____

   b) dissolved sugar and water _____

   c) sand and water _____

filtering
sieving
evaporating

5. Name **two** solids not mentioned in question 4 that you could separate with a **sieve**. _____

6. Name one **mixture** not mentioned in question 4 that you could separate using **filter paper**. _____

7. Name one **dissolved** solid not mentioned in question 4 that could be separated from water by **evaporating**. _____

Test it

Mrs Twigg's class use the Internet to e-mail a school overseas. They often swap accounts of their experiments and what they have found out. Here is Josh's latest report.

Hi Tomas.

Yesterday, Mrs Twigg let us use thermometers for the very first time. She **explained** to us that **temperature** is a **measure** of how hot or cold something is, and that it is measured in **degrees Celsius (°C)** using an **instrument** called a **thermometer**.

We had to **compare** the temperature of the water in five different beakers and then decide which was the hottest.

I have done some thermometer drawings and scanned them into the computer to show you the temperature reading of the water in each beaker. The drawings are not very good. I hope you can read them all right.

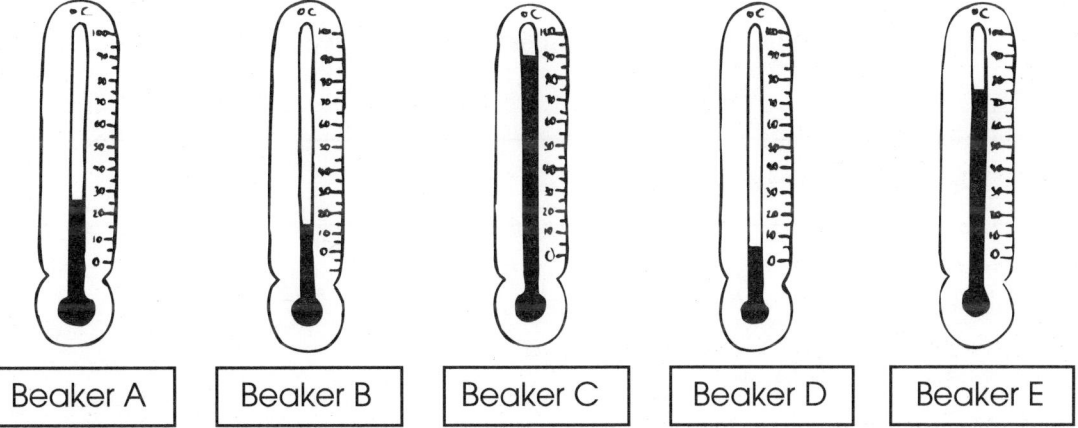

| Beaker A | Beaker B | Beaker C | Beaker D | Beaker E |

Then we went outside into the playground to measure the **air temperature** in shadow and in bright sunlight. These are the temperatures we measured:

| shadow | 14°C |

| sunlight | 23°C |

Then it rained, so we returned quickly to the classroom to **record** our results.

What is the **air temperature** outside the place where you live?

Goodbye for now, Josh

Photocopiable

Test it

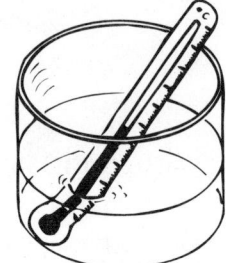

1. Answer these questions with full sentences.

a) What is **temperature**?

_____

_____

b) What **units** is **temperature** measured in?

_____

2. Arrange the beakers of water shown in the text in order of **temperature**.

Coldest   Hottest

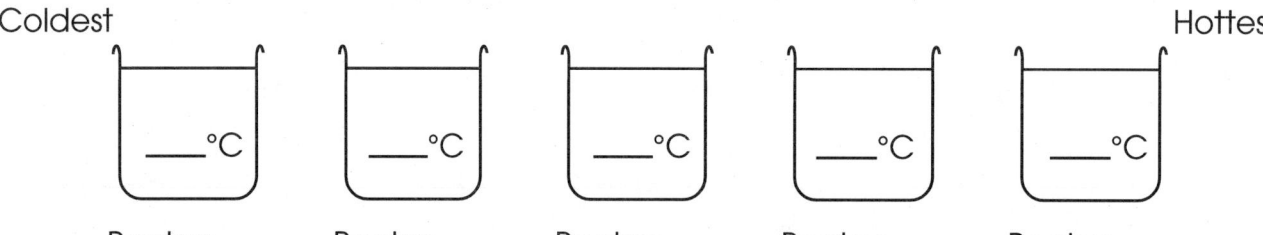

Beaker ___   Beaker ___   Beaker ___   Beaker ___   Beaker ___

3. Why did the children go out into the playground?

_____

_____

4. How many **degrees** warmer was the air

in sunlight than the air in shadow? _____ °C

5. What would happen to the **temperature** of the water in the five beakers if they were left standing in the classroom for 24 hours?

_____

_____

With a friend, measure the **air temperature** in the same place outdoors every **hour** through the school day. Record each time and temperature like this:

time: _____

temp: _____°C

Now display your findings on a line graph.

Test it

1. Use words from the box below to complete each sentence.

   a) **Temperature** is a measure of how _____ or _____ something is.

   b) _____ is measured in _____ **Celsius**.

   c) A _____ is used to measure **temperature**.

   | cold | thermometer | hot | degrees | Temperature |

2. How many different beakers of water did Josh have to find the **temperature** of? _____

3. Which beaker had the **hottest** water in it? Write the letter. _____

   What was the **temperature** of this water? _____ °C

   Which beaker contained the **coldest** water? _____

   The **temperature** of this water was _____ °C

4. Why did Josh and his friends go outside into the playground?

   _____

   _____

5. What did Josh and his friends do when they went back into the classroom?

   _____

   _____

6. What was the difference in **temperature** between the **hottest** and the **coldest** water samples? _____ °C

With a friend, measure the **air temperature** in the same place outdoors every hour through the school day. Record each measurement like this:

time: _____
temp: _____ °C

Make a chart of the results.

Soaking it up

You are going to **compare** different kinds of paper to find out which is best for **soaking** up water. The paper that is most **absorbent** will soak up water best.

What you need: a measuring jug, a timer, some water, a tray (such as a seed tray without holes in) and several sheets of these types of paper: sugar paper, writing paper, newspaper, paper towels, pages from a glossy magazine. All the sheets should measure about 20cm × 30cm (A4 size).

What to do:

1. Measure 50ml of water in a measuring jug.

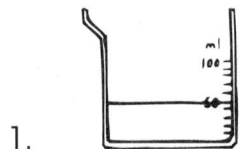
1.

2. Put one crumpled sheet of sugar paper into the water.

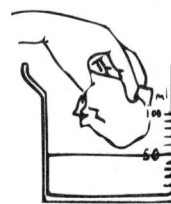
2.

3. Leave the paper in the water for 30 seconds.

3.

4. Take the paper out and place it in the tray. Do not squeeze it!

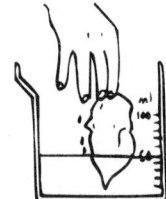
4.

5. Repeat the process with more sheets of sugar paper until all the water has been **absorbed**.

6. Write your result in the correct place on the chart below.

7. Do the **experiment** four more times, using a different type of paper each time.

8. Remember to write your result on the chart after testing each type of paper.

9. Answer this question. Write on the back of this sheet.
- Do you think this is a **fair test**?
- Give reasons for your answer.

Paper type	Number of sheets to soak up all the water
sugar	
writing	
newspaper	
towel	
glossy	

Testing tights

Kylie and Rebecca had five pairs of tights, all of equal length. They wanted to find out which pair was the most **stretchy**.

To make a **fair test**, they used the same mass to stretch each pair of tights. They made careful measurements of length to make sure their results would be correct.

This bar graph shows what they found out. Use it to answer the questions at the bottom of the page.

Bar graph to show stretchiness of tights

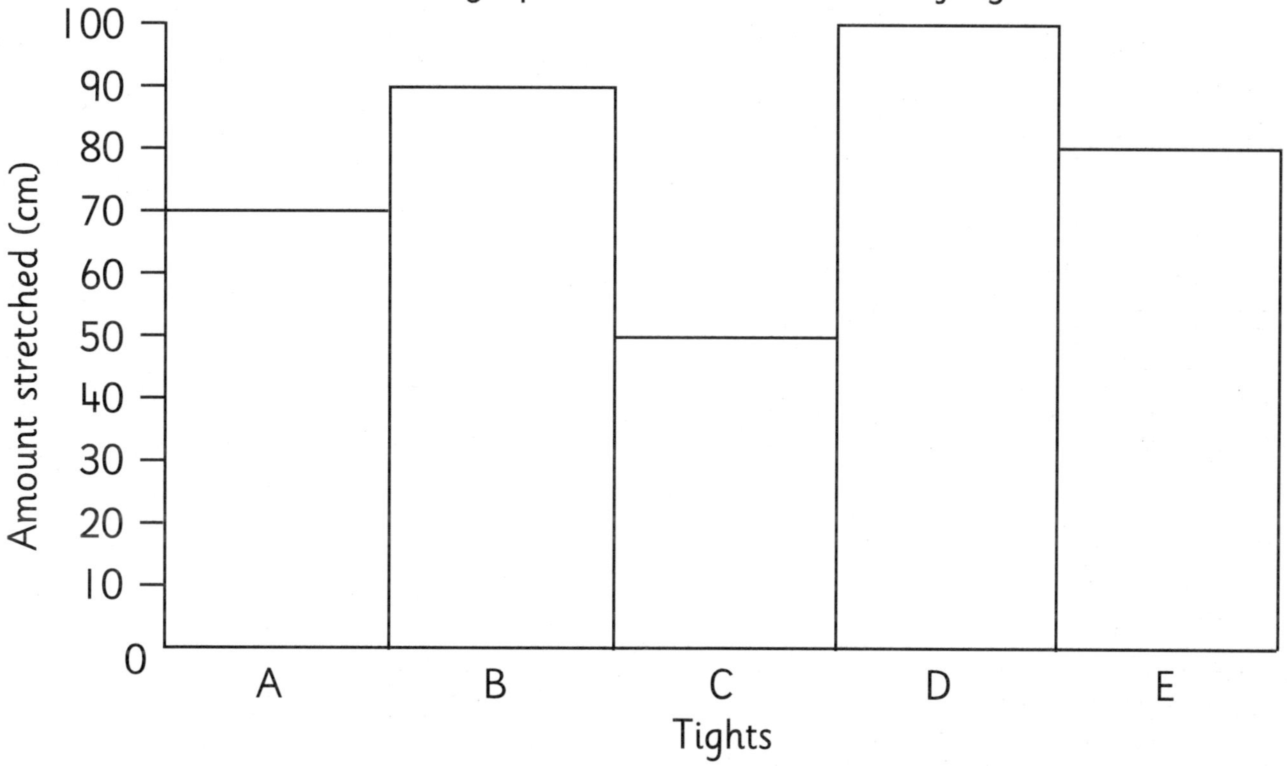

(Bar graph: A = 70, B = 90, C = 50, D = 100, E = 80; y-axis: Amount stretched (cm); x-axis: Tights)

1. Which tights stretched the **most**? ☐
2. Which tights stretched the **least**? ☐
3. Which tights stretched 10cm more than pair E? ☐
4. Which tights stretched exactly 20cm less than pair B? ☐
5. Arrange the tights in order of stretchiness, starting with the pair that stretched the most.

MOST ☐ ☐ ☐ ☐ ☐ LEAST

A material test

Sort each set of materials and write their names in the correct boxes.

1.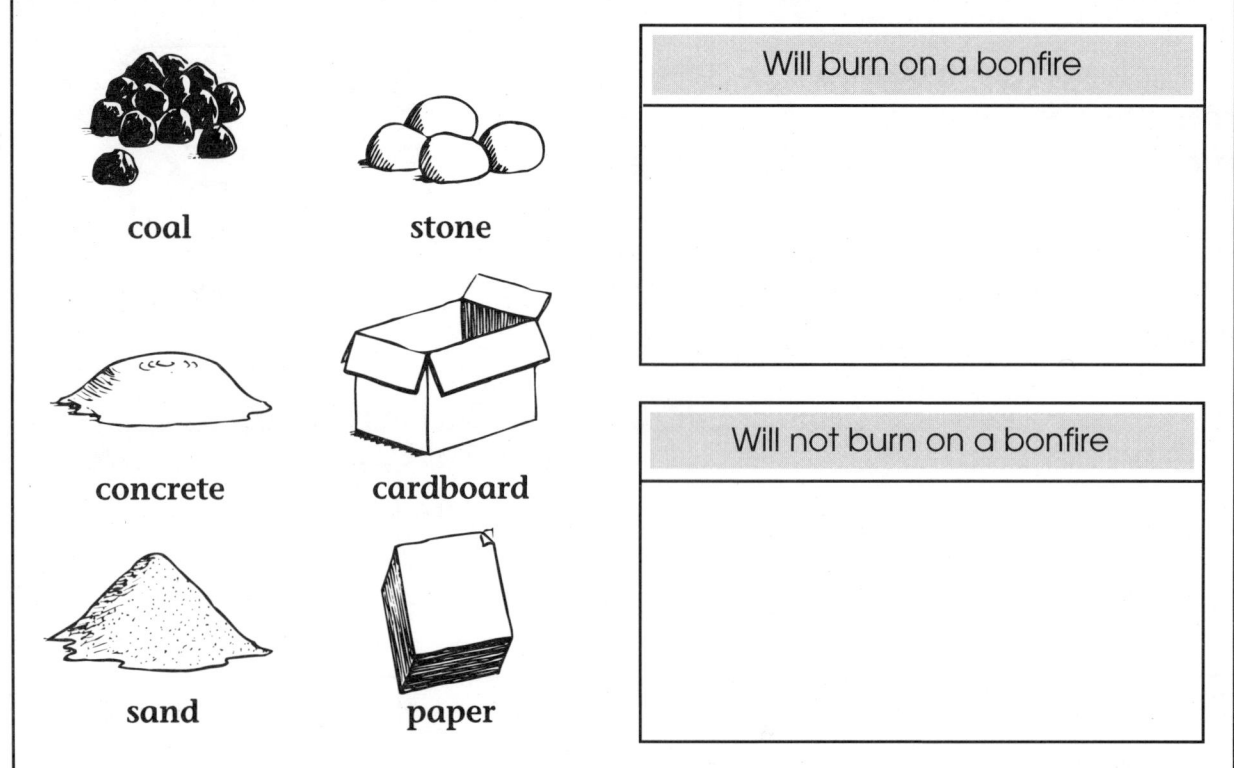

2.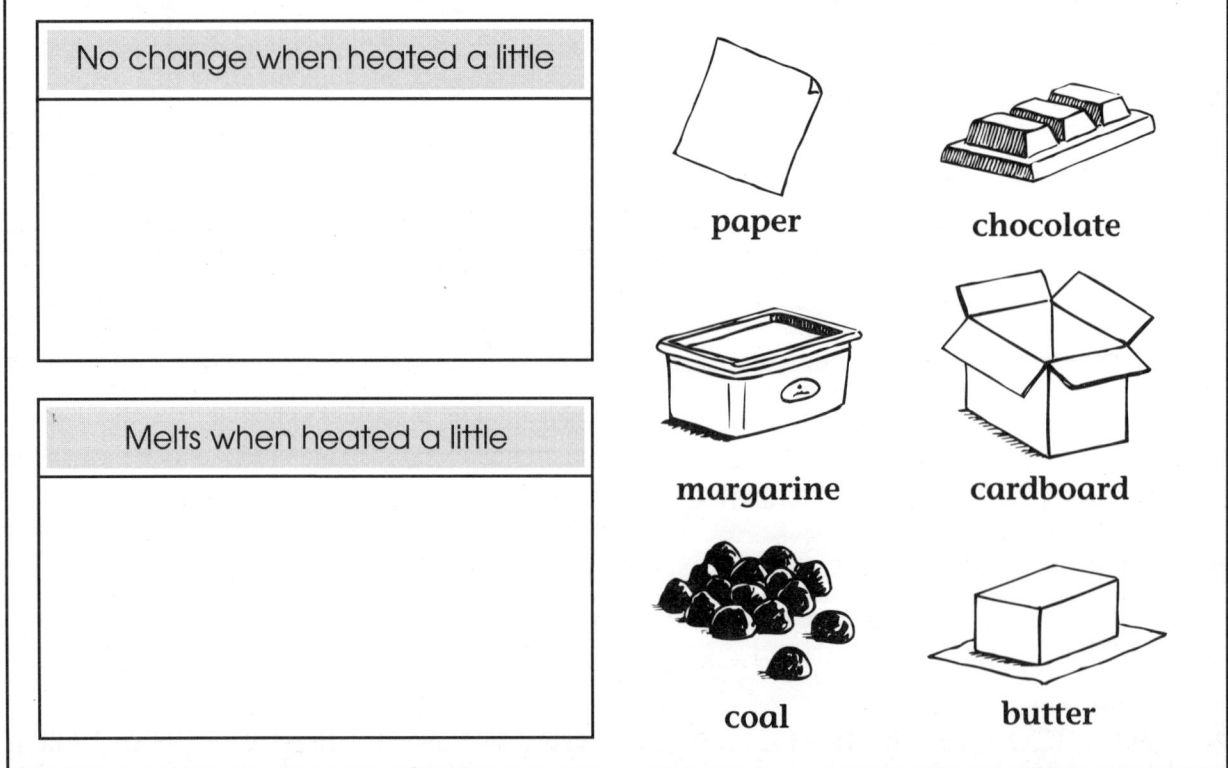

3. In each box, write the name of one other material not mentioned on this page that can be grouped with the materials already there.

Water and the water cycle

The **water cycle** is the movement of water around the Earth. It has been going on for millions of years.
The water cycle has five main stages:

1. Heat from the Sun causes water in seas and lakes to **evaporate** and become a gas. This gas is called **water vapour**.
2. As water vapour rises into the sky, it cools and **condenses** to form **clouds**. Clouds are made up of tiny **droplets** of water.
3. The clouds are blown by the wind over the land.
4. When clouds reach a hill or a mountain, the water in them often starts to fall as **rain**. Sometimes, if it is very cold, the water in the clouds will **freeze** and fall to the ground as **hail**, **snow** or **sleet**.
5. The rain collects in rivers and streams and flows back to the sea, where the whole process begins all over again.

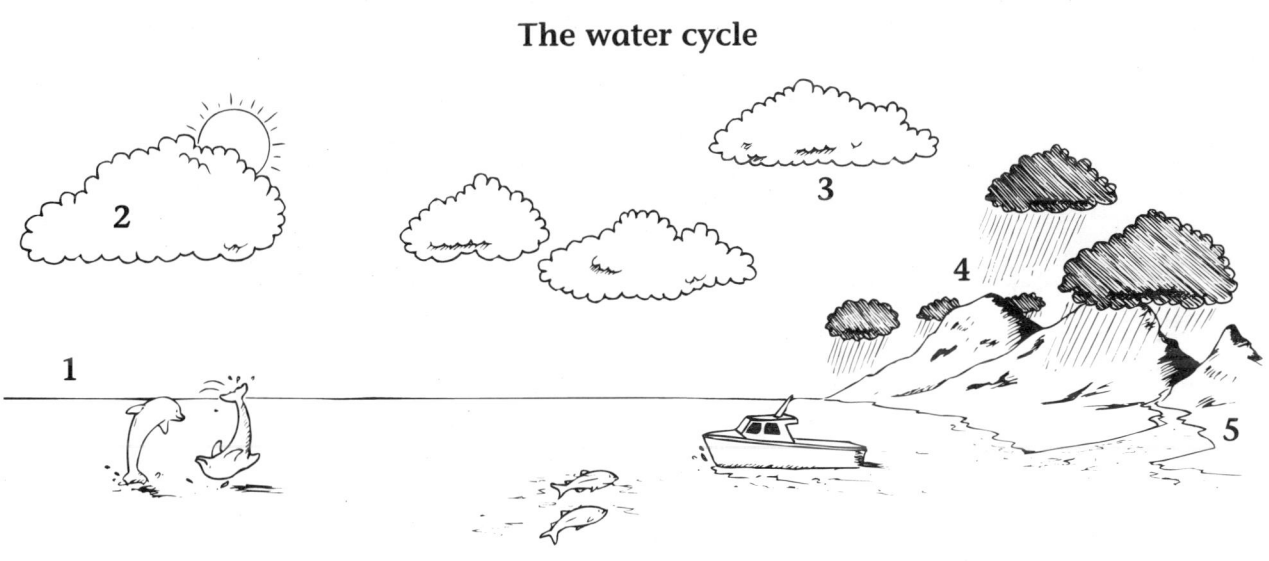

The water cycle

Some of the rain water **soaks** into the ground. Part of this water is taken in by plants through their roots and released through their leaves as water vapour.

Water and the water cycle

1. Answer these questions with complete sentences.
a) What is the **water cycle**?

_____

b) What happens to **water vapour** as it rises in the sky?

_____

c) What are **clouds** made up of?

_____

2. Name three forms of water that fall from clouds.

_____   _____   _____

3. True or false? Circle the correct answer.
a) Some rain water is taken in by plants through their leaves. **True / False**

b) The roots of plants release water vapour into the air. **True / False**

4. Cross out the words that are wrong.
When water **evaporates**, it changes into a **solid / liquid / gas**.

5. How does most rain water get back to the sea?

_____

6. What happens to some of the water that **soaks** into the ground?

_____

_____

 7. Look up the meaning of the word **condense** and write it down.

_____

 On another sheet of paper, draw a large labelled diagram to show how water gets from the sea to the land and back again. Ask your teacher if you can display your diagram.

Water and the water cycle

1. Complete these sentences.

   a) The _____ _____ is the movement of water around the Earth.

   b) As water vapour rises in the sky, it cools and _____ to form _____.

   c) Clouds are made up of tiny _____ of water.

2. Which of these are forms of water? Tick the correct boxes.

   soak ☐   hail ☐   rain ☐
   sleet ☐   cycle ☐   snow ☐

3. Where does most water **evaporate** from to form **clouds**? _____

4. What does most rain water flow in to get back to the sea? _____

5. Plants take in water through their roots. Which part of a plant does water escape from? _____

6. Look up the meaning of the word **evaporate** and write it down.

   _____

7. Study the **diagram** of the **water cycle** carefully. Now write these words in the correct order to follow the water cycle, starting with **evaporate**.

   wind   river   evaporate   rain   cloud

   _____

Ask your teacher for a copy of 'The water cycle' sheet. Fill in the label boxes. Ask your teacher if you can display your labelled diagram.

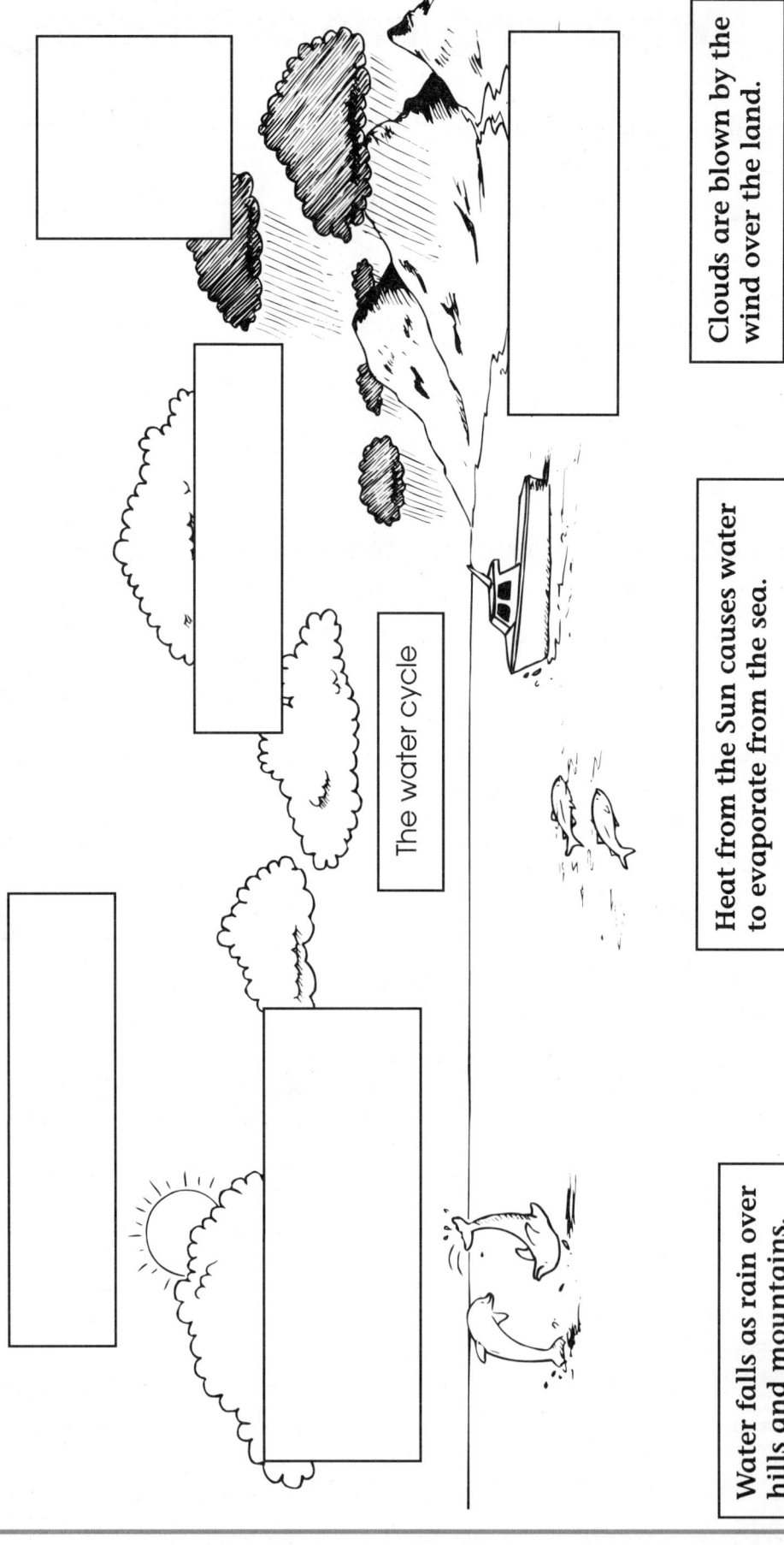

Evaporating and condensing

The missing words in the text below are listed in the box on the right. Write the number of the correct word in each gap in the text. The first one has been done for you.

Evaporating

__3__ is changing into water vapour all the time. We say it is evaporating. The ____ the water, the more quickly it ____. When it is ____, the water is evaporating as quickly as it can. Water evaporates from the surfaces of ____ and lakes. Some water evaporates from the surfaces of animals and plants. Some water evaporates from dead things. When water evaporates from dead things, they ____ up. When water evaporates from any ____, the rest of the mixture is left behind. This is why ____ is left when sea-water evaporates from a rock pool.

1	warmer
2	mixture
3	~~water~~
4	evaporates
5	salt
6	dry
7	boiling
8	seas

Condensing

1	dew
2	droplets
3	colder
4	cold
5	morning
6	air
7	warm
8	condensing

The warmer the ____ is, the more water vapour it can hold. If warm air becomes ____ enough, some of the water vapour it contains changes into tiny ____ of water. When this happens, we say the water vapour is ____. If ____ air touches a cold surface, drops of water form on the surface. This happens on the outside of a glass tumbler that contains an ice-cold drink. ____ on grass and other outdoor plants in the early ____ is also caused by water vapour condensing on surfaces that are ____ than the air.

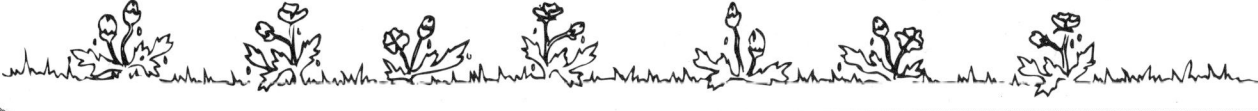

Photocopiable

1 Dirty water

These pictures show four different kinds of **water pollution**. Choose the right title for each picture from the list at the bottom of the page. Write the correct title in the box underneath each picture.

Factory waste flowing into a river
An oil spill at sea
Acid rain damaging forest trees
Household rubbish dumped in a pond

Can you think of any other ways in which water can be **polluted**? Write your ideas on the back of this sheet.

COVER THESE INSTRUCTIONS WHEN PHOTOCOPYING.

Notes for the teacher:
Enlarge to A3 size. As an alternative, a more difficult version of this sheet is provided on page 87.

Dirty water

These pictures show four different kinds of water **pollution**.
Below each picture, write what is causing the pollution.
The words in the box at the bottom of the page will be useful.

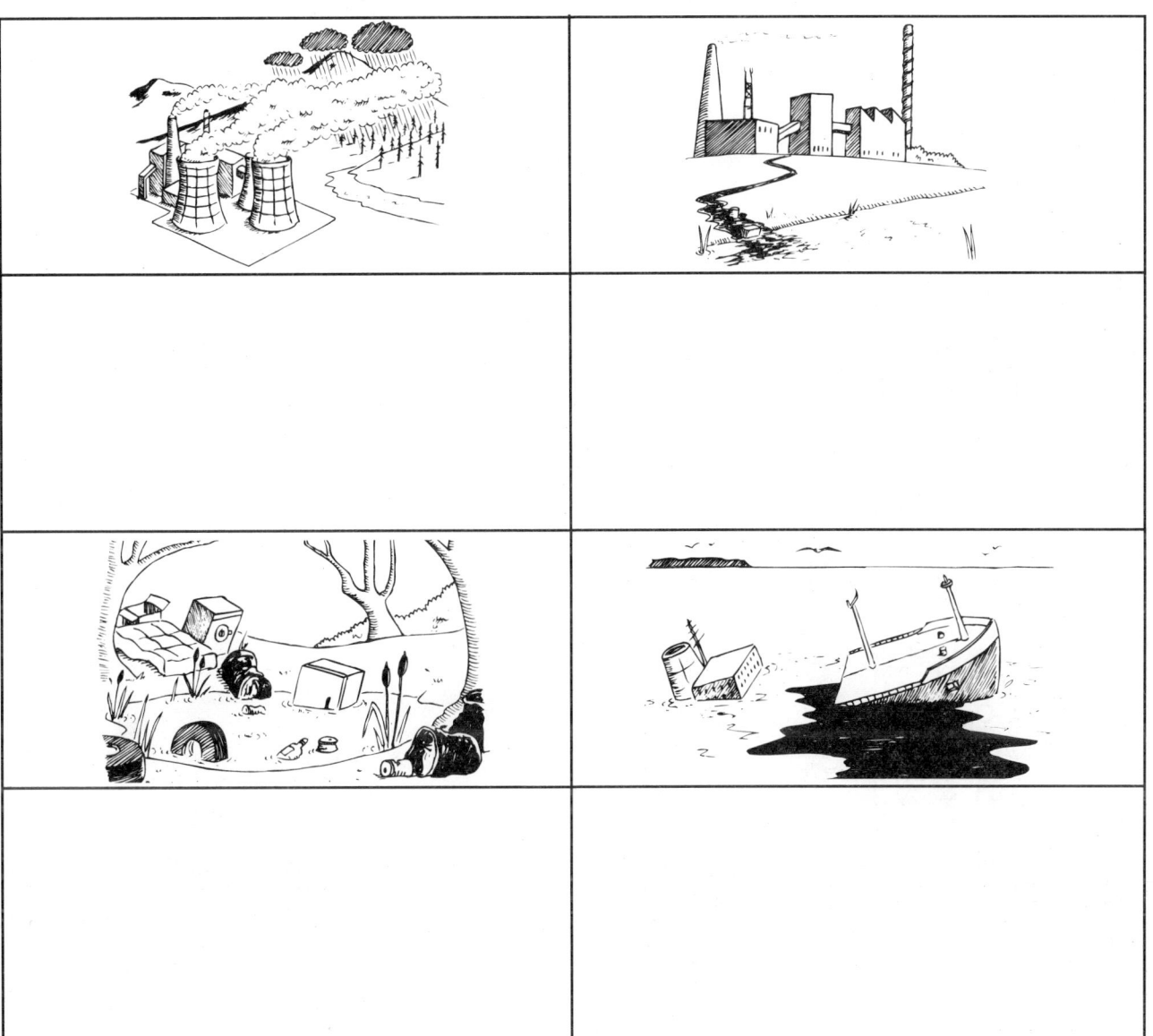

| factory | oil | acid rain | pond | waste |
| river | rubbish | sea | forest | damage |

Can you think of any other ways in which water can be **polluted**?
Write your ideas on the back of this sheet.

Notes for the teacher:
Enlarge to A3 size. As an alternative, a less difficult version of this sheet is provided on page 86.

Photocopiable

Save it

Design a poster with pictures and text telling people how to **conserve** water. Include these words in the writing on your poster: **waste, save, tap, off, hosepipe, water, drought, running**. When you have finished, cut out your poster and ask your teacher if you can display it somewhere in school.

HOW TO SAVE WATER

Enlarge to A3 size.

Solids and liquids

A material that is **solid** has a fixed **volume** and a fixed **shape**. A **solid** does not change shape when you move it. **Wood**, **stone** and **plastic** are examples of solids.

Solids have a fixed shape and volume.

A material that is **liquid** has a fixed volume but no fixed shape. The shape of a **liquid** changes to fit the shape of the container that holds it. **Water**, **cooking oil** and **shampoo** are liquids.

When solids or liquids are gently heated, they **expand**. When solids or liquids are gently cooled, they **contract**. Liquids expand and contract more than solids when heated or cooled by the same amount.

Liquids have no fixed shape.

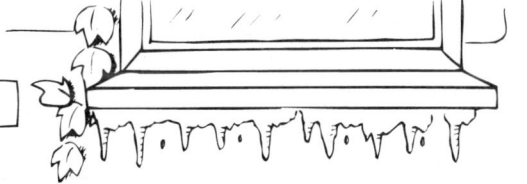

Solids can melt and liquids can freeze.

Most solids will change into liquids if heated to a high enough **temperature**. This is called **melting**. Most liquids will change into solids if cooled to a low enough temperature. This is called **freezing**.

Some solids behave like liquids in the way they move. Liquids **flow** and can be **poured** from one container to another. **Salt**, **rice** and **sand** are examples of solids that will also flow and pour. They do so because their particles are very small and move easily over each other.

Some solids behave like liquids.

Solids and liquids

1. What is the difference between a **solid** and a **liquid**?

   _____

   _____

   _____

   _____

2. Answer these questions with complete sentences.
   What happens to **solids** and **liquids** when they are gently heated?

   _____

   Which will **contract** more with the same amount of cooling, a **solid** or a **liquid**?

   _____

3. What causes **solids** to **melt**? _____

4. What causes **liquids** to **freeze**? _____

5. Why do solids such as **salt**, **rice** and **sand** flow and pour like liquids?

   _____

6. Name any other **solids** you know that will **flow** and **pour** like **liquids**.

   _____

7. Find out and write down the meanings of these words:

   volume: _____

   expand: _____

   contract: _____

On another sheet of paper, draw two boxes. Label one box **solids** and the other box **liquids**. Sort these materials and write their names in the correct boxes.

| coal | chalk | petrol | hair | orange juice |
| cola | gold | vinegar | sugar | milk |

Can you think of any other materials to add to each box?

Solids and liquids

1. Complete these sentences.

   a) A material that is **solid** has _____

   _____

   b) A material that is **liquid** _____

   _____

2. Circle the correct answer.
   a) **Wood**, **shampoo** and **plastic** are all solids. **True / False**

   b) **Cooking oil** and **water** are liquids. **True / False**

3. What is it called when a **solid** changes into a **liquid**? _____

4. What is it called when a **liquid** changes into a **solid**? _____

5. Name three solids that will **flow** and **pour**. _____

6. Tick the **solid** materials in this list.

   aluminium ☐   milk ☐   brick ☐

   lemonade ☐   feathers ☐   sponge ☐

7. Find out and write down the meanings of these words:

   a) volume: _____

   b) expand: _____

   c) contract: _____

On another sheet of paper, draw two boxes. Label one box **solids** and the other box **liquids**. Sort these materials and write their names in the correct boxes.

| coal | chalk | petrol | hair | orange juice |
| cola | gold | vinegar | sugar | milk |

Photocopiable

Solids and liquids pictures

You will need: a copy of the 'Solids and liquids chart', scissors, glue.

Instructions:
1. Cut carefully around each picture and each label.
2. Stick each picture into the correct column on the chart.
3. Stick the correct label in the box below each picture.

 milk	 brick	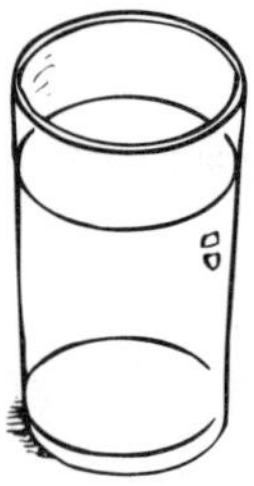 lemonade
 metal	 glass	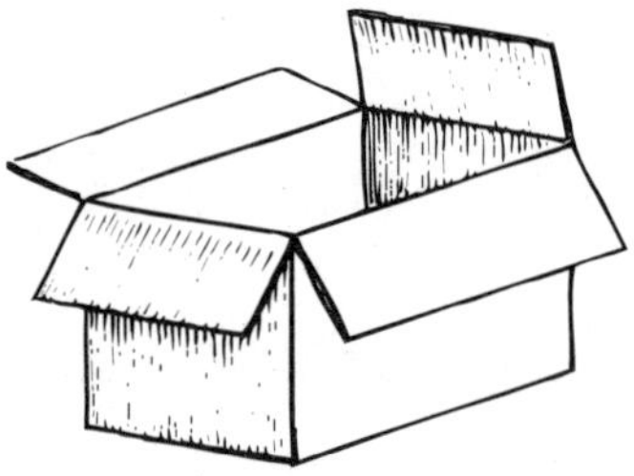 cardboard
 vinegar	 oil	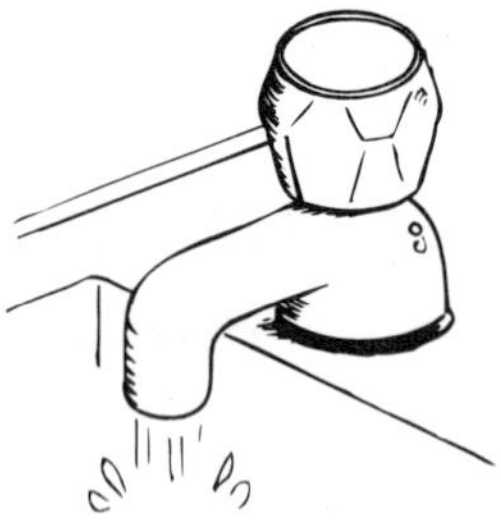 water
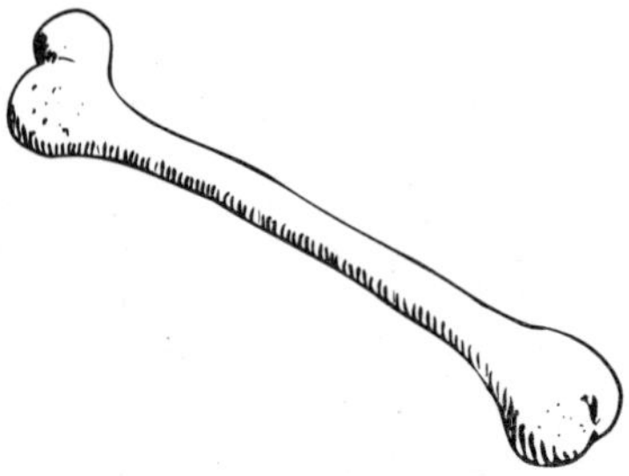 bone	 leather	 petrol

SCHOLASTIC DEVELOPING SCIENCE LANGUAGE for Materials with 8–9 year olds

Solids and liquids chart

Name _____ Class _____

| solids | liquids |

Enlarge to A3 size.

Solids and liquids round-the-class game

Question	Answer
* Any material with a fixed size and shape.	liquid
Liquid fuel for vehicles.	solid
A solid that can be poured like a liquid.	petrol
A drink with a fizz.	sand
Fibre from the fleece of an animal.	lemonade
A solid from trees.	wool
A colourless, tasteless liquid with no smell.	wood
A soft modelling material.	water
A good liquid for frying chips in.	play dough
Water in solid form.	cooking oil
What a cow produces.	ice
Any material with a fixed size but no fixed shape.	milk

COVER THESE INSTRUCTIONS WHEN PHOTOCOPYING.

Teacher instructions

Photocopy this sheet onto card. Cut along the dotted lines. Fold each card in half along the solid line with the text on the outside. Fasten with tape or glue.

If you are working with a small group, give each child a card. If you are working with the whole class, share the cards out one between two or three. All the cards must be given out.

The child (or group) with the card marked * reads the question aloud. The child with the answer to that question reads it out, then reads out the question on the back of the card. This goes on until the first child has read out the answer on his or her card.

What are solids, liquids and gases?

All materials are solids, liquids or gases.
Solids have a definite shape and size.
Liquids have a fixed size but no fixed shape.
Liquids will take the shape of the container into which they are placed.
Gases have neither a fixed size nor a fixed shape.
Gases will completely fill any space they enter.

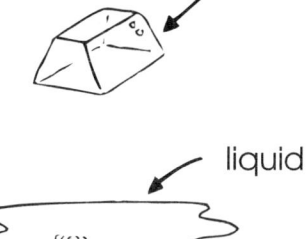

1. Which kind of material has:

a) neither a fixed size nor a fixed shape? _____

b) a fixed size but no fixed shape? _____

c) a definite size and shape? _____

2. Tick the correct column for each material.

	solid	liquid	gas
wood			
vapour			
oil			
water			

	solid	liquid	gas
milk			
air			
rock			
sugar			

3. Write in the missing words in these sentences.

Water _____ is water in the form of a **gas**.

_____ is water in **solid** form.

4. On the back of this sheet, write the names of six **solids**, six **liquids** and six **gases** that are not mentioned on this sheet. Use reference books to help you.

Uses of solids, liquids and gases

1. Connect each of these **solids** to its most likely uses.

metal		clothing, curtains, carpets
plastic		water pipes, radiators, saucepans, hammer heads
fabric		washing-up bowls, saucepan handles

2. Write the names of three **solid** materials that can be used for building a house. Then write which part of the house each material would be used for.

a)	
b)	
c)	

Why would each material be used where it was?

a) _____

b) _____

c) _____

3. Write **three** ways in which water is used in your home.
Water is used in our home for

a) _____ b) _____ c) _____

4. Circle the activities that could not be done without a special supply of air.

travelling in a submarine   riding a horse   surfing

cycling   travelling in space   deep sea diving